HANDWRITING LINK

An evidence-based approach to an integrated literacy program

Year 1 Workbook

Carol A. Christensen and Glenn A. Christensen

Production staff
Graphics/Layout: Dean Maynard
Publisher: Rob Watts

Knowledge Books and Software
ABN 75003053316
PO Box 50, Sandgate, Queensland 4017
Phone: (07) 5568 0288
Fax: (07) 5568 0277
Email: orders@kbs.com.au
Website: www.kbs.com.au

Printed in Australia

Product code: E532

ISBN: 9781921016448

Table of Contents

Blank page intentionally added.

Background and Directions for Implementing the Program.

Handwriting LINK is based on research into the most effective approaches to teaching handwriting. This research shows that proficiency in handwriting can have a dramatic impact on children's abilities to create high quality written text.

The approach to handwriting taken in **Handwriting LINK** is dramatically different from traditional approaches to teaching handwriting. It is essential for teachers to read the *Teacher's Version* of each workbook to implement this innovative approach to handwriting with maximum effectiveness.

This workbook is suitable for children in *Year* 1 who have completed **Handwriting LINK**, *Book 1*.

Directions for Implementing the Program.

Writing Bubble Letters

1. **Use a developmental sequence**

Teachers should ensure that children are at an appropriate developmental level before introducing handwriting. Begin with phonological awareness. Phonological awareness refers to the ability to hear the sounds in spoken language. In particular, children should be able to hear rhymes and initial sounds in words. Children also need to know letter-sounds correspondences. If children cannot rhyme, identify initial sounds and identify the sounds that letters represent, then they are not ready to begin handwriting. Time should be taken to teach these skills and when they are mastered, writing letters can begin.

2. **Teacher demonstration to introduce letters one at a time**.

The first step in each lesson in this workbook is teacher demonstration. When teaching how to write letters, teachers should focus on developing fluency and proficiency as well as promoting children's ability to recall letter-shapes from memory. First demonstrate how to write each letter by making the letter in the air and writing it on a white board.

3. **Provide extended practice in making letter shapes** using large fluid movements. Give children time to practise making the letter using a variety of activities. These would include:

- Writing letters in the air
- Writing on a flat surface (eg desks)
- Finger painting letters
- Tracing letters on sandpaper shapes
- Writing letters in sand

4. **Introduce writing each letter in workbooks using rainbow letters in bubble shapes**.

- Children select four coloured pencils
- Children write rainbow letters within the bubble shape. They should begin at the green dot, follow the directional arrow and stop at the red dot.
- When guiding students strokes, teachers should provide short verbal cues.

Writing Letters on a Single Line

1. **Teachers' Demonstration**. When children have been introduced to all letters using bubble letters they can complete activities with letters on a single line. The focus should continue to be on teaching children fluency in production of letters and for children to recall the shapes from memory. The single line should be seen as a guide for placement of the letter, not as a mechanism to restrict fluency in creating the shape. Teachers should demonstrate how to write the letter on a single line by writing it repeatedly on a whiteboard.

2. **Children Practise Letter Shapes** using large fluid movements. Give children practice in making the letter using a variety of activities. These would include:

- Writing letters in the air
- Writing on a flat surface (eg desks)
- Writing letters on a whiteboard.

3. **Children complete page in Workbook**. Children should write letter shapes in the bubble letter and then complete each line in the workbook.

Writing Letters on a Double Lines

When children have completed all the single-line pages in the workbook, they will be ready to begin writing within double lines. At this stage, children should have mastery of making the shape and are ready to focus on fitting the letter using the constraints of the lines. The same steps should be followed as in completing other activities in the workbook:

1. **Teacher's demonstration.**
2. **Children practise letter shapes**
3. **Children complete page in workbook**

Bubble Letters

Blank page intentionally added.

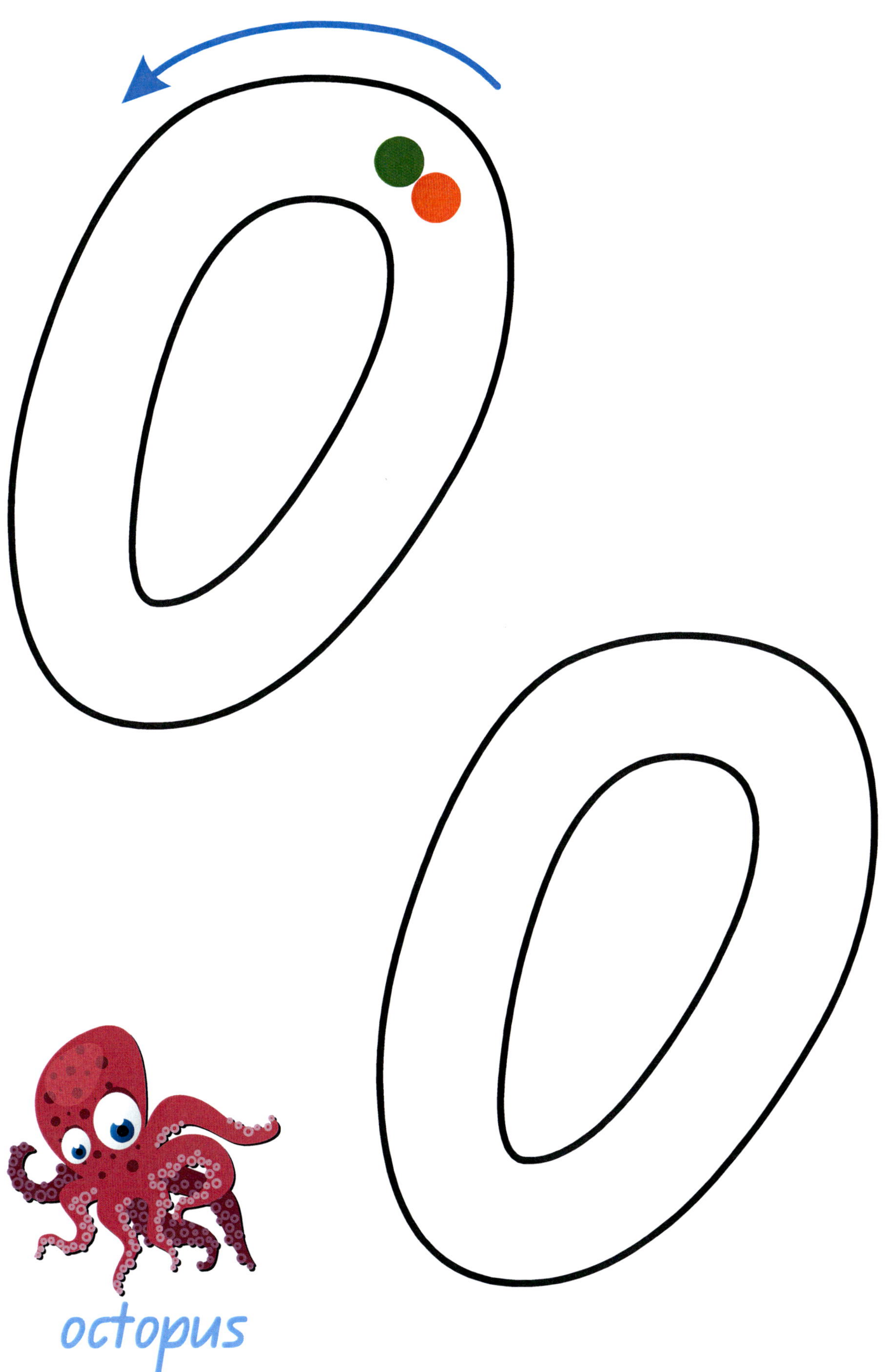

octopus

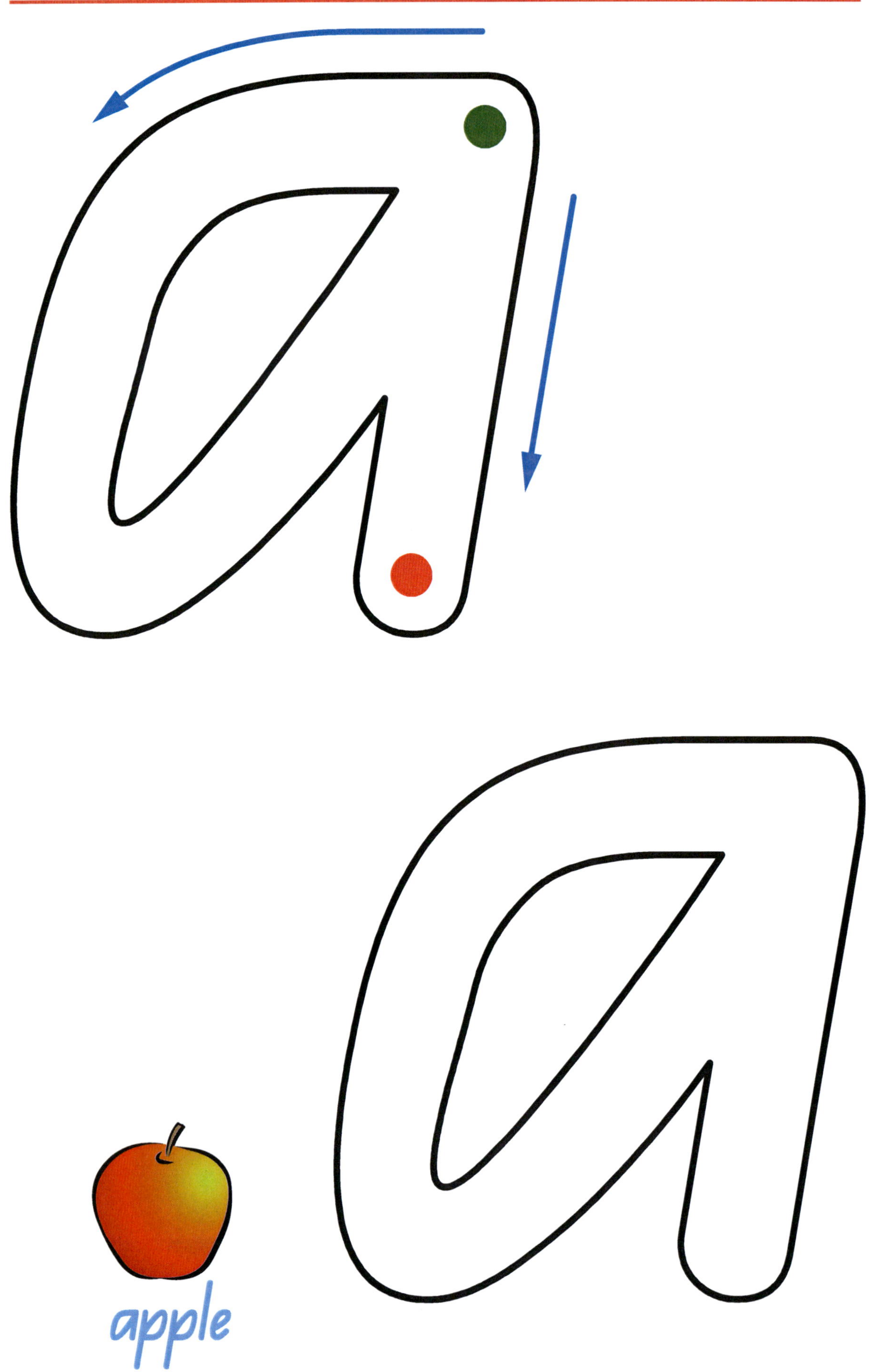
apple

dog

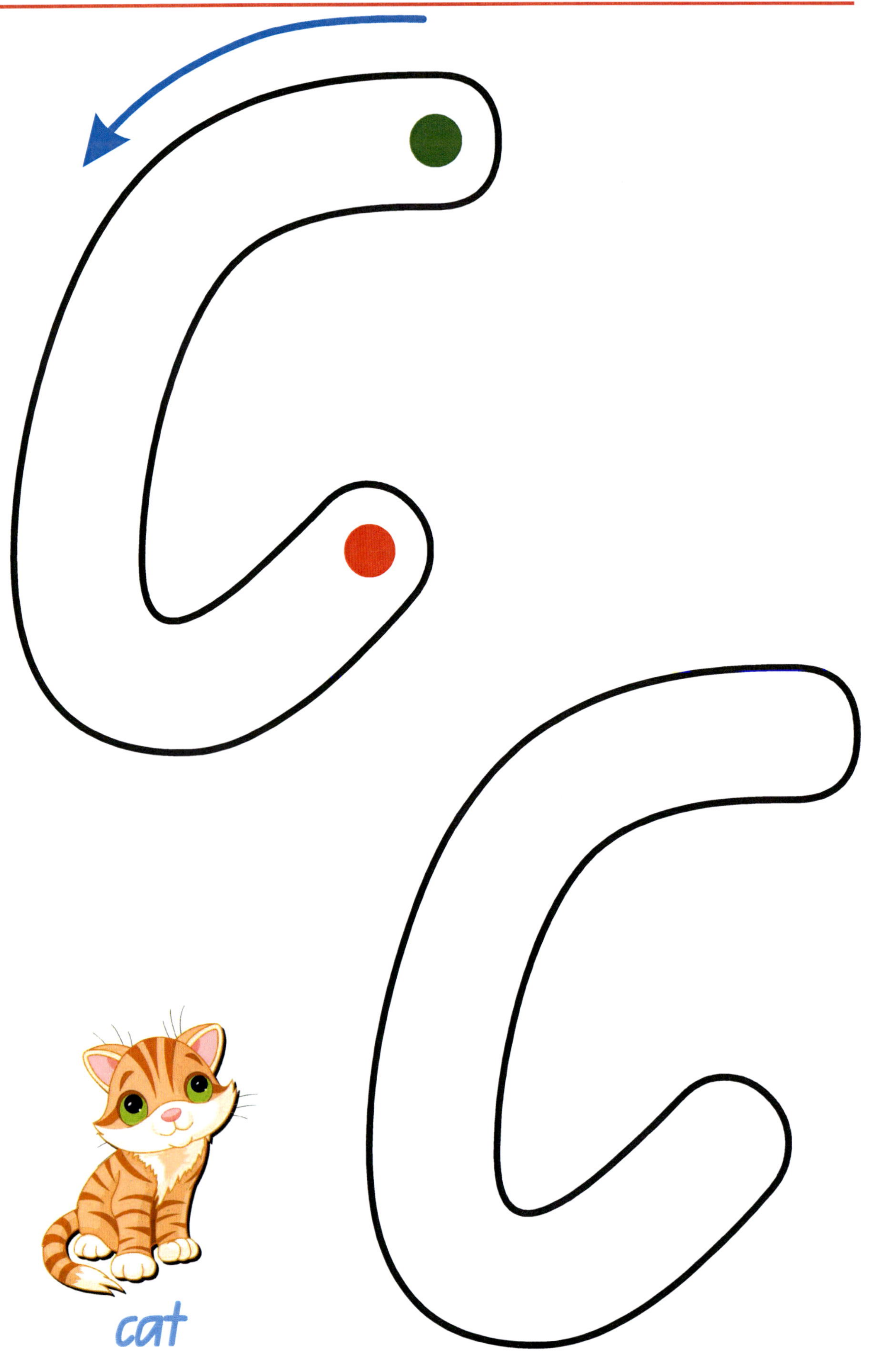
cat

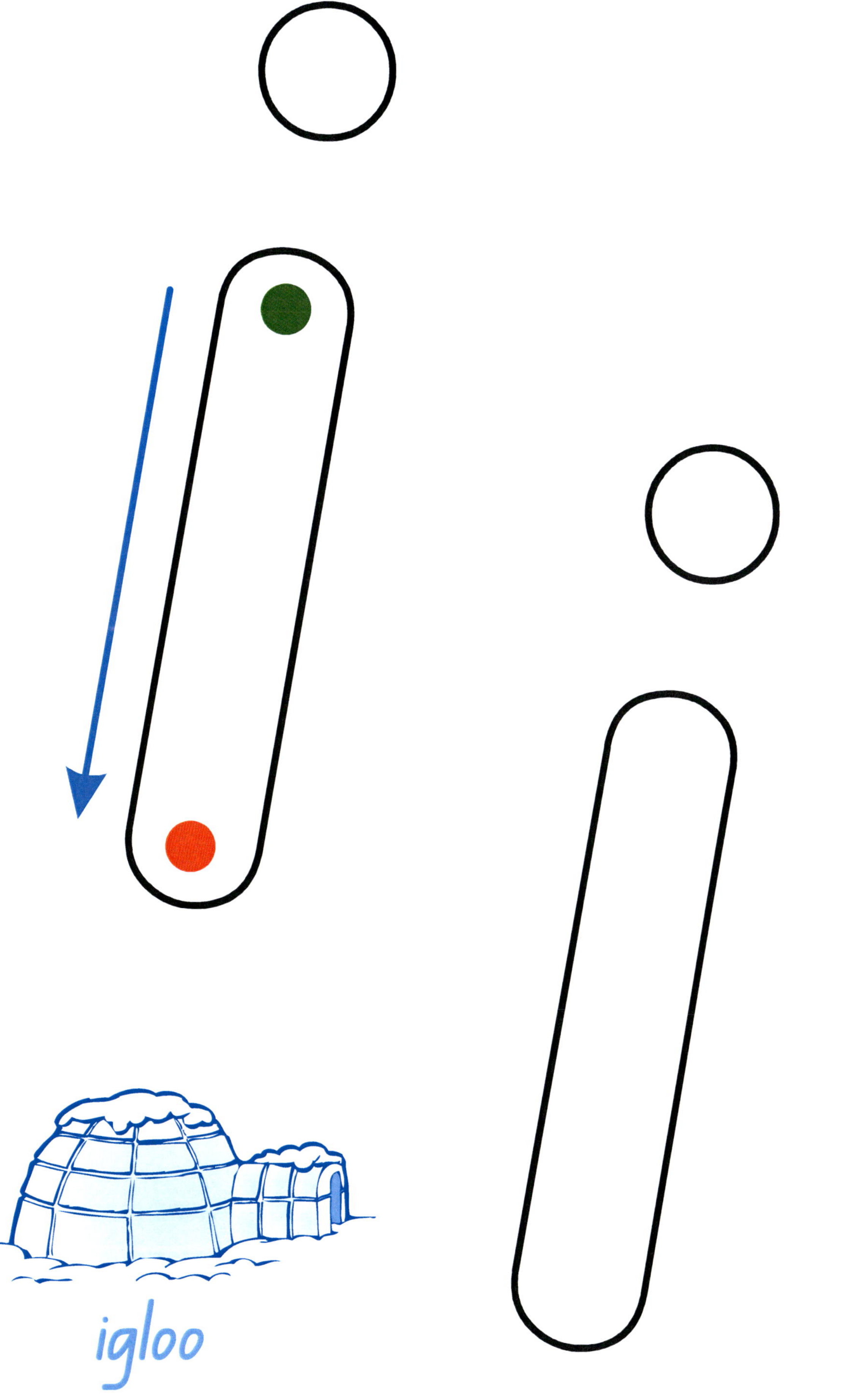
igloo

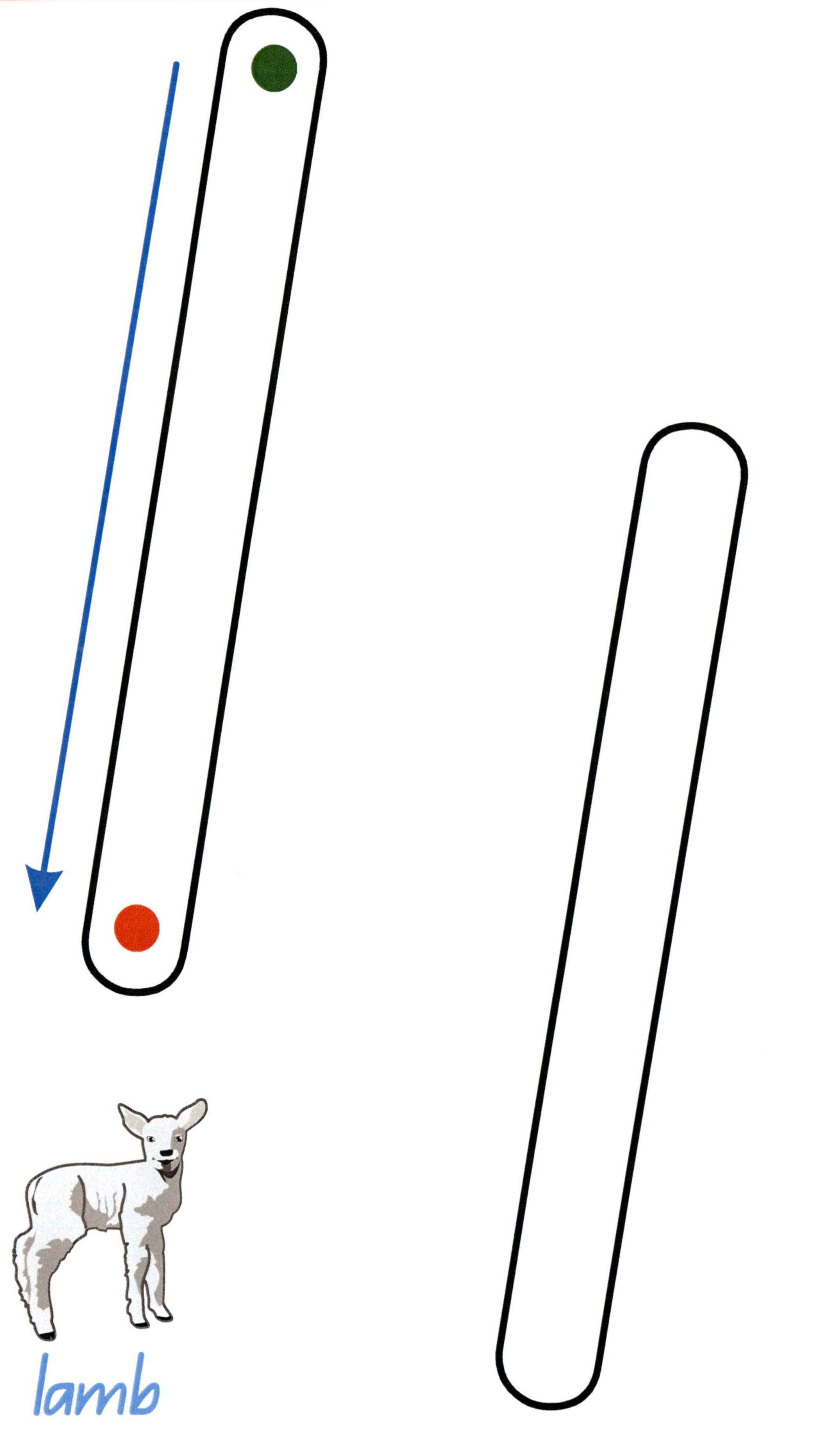
lamb

tiger

moon

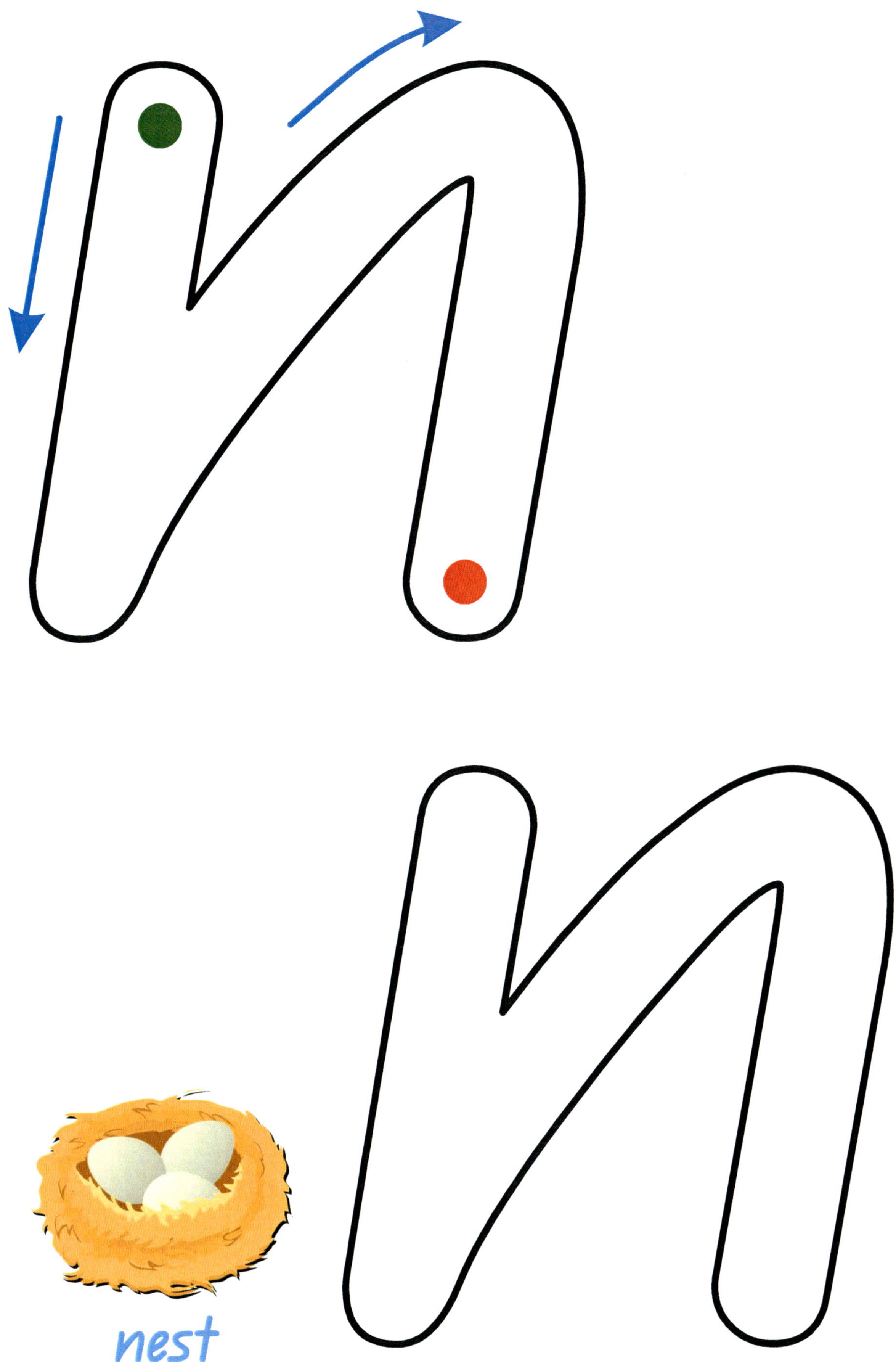
nest

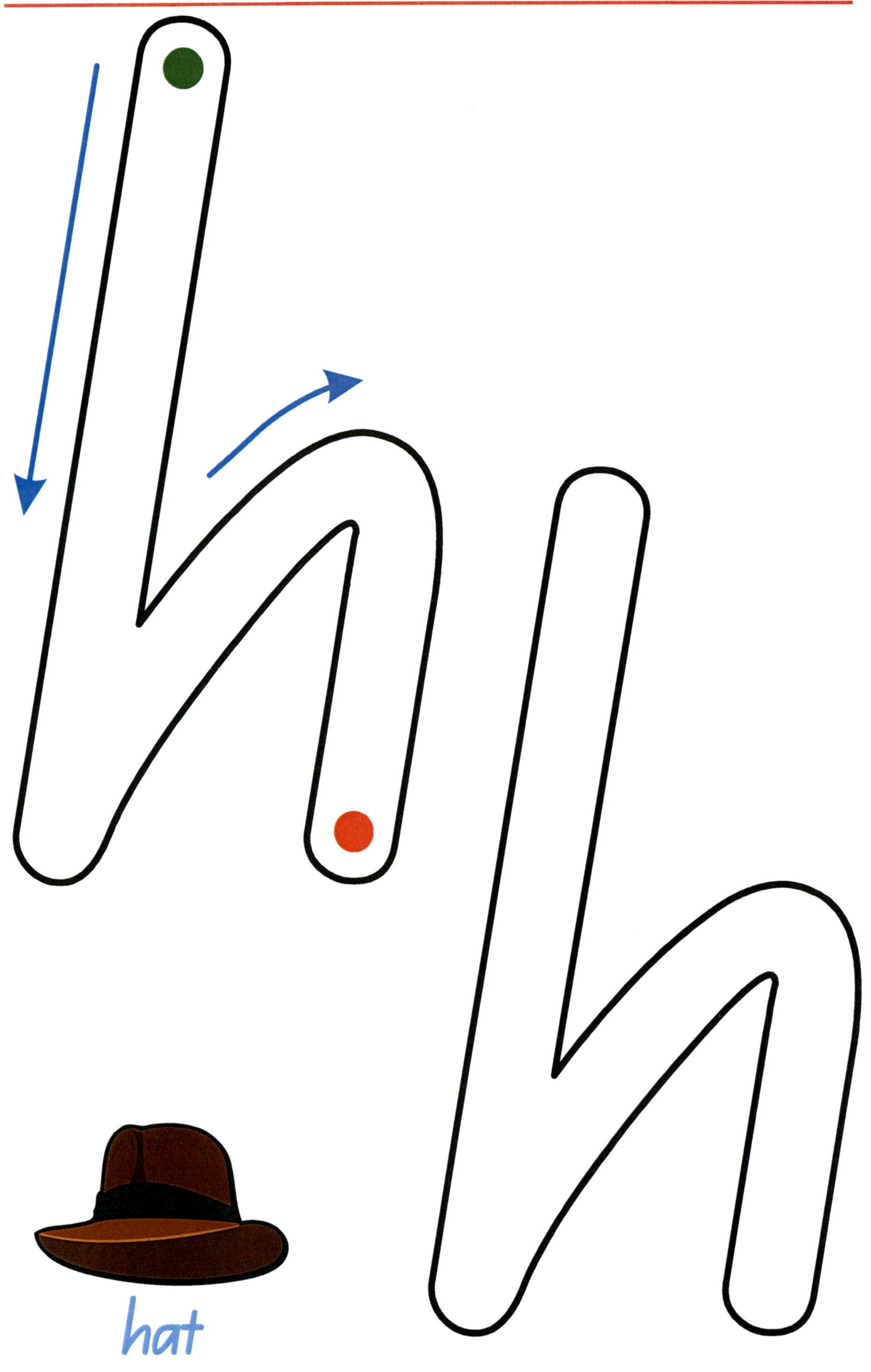
hat

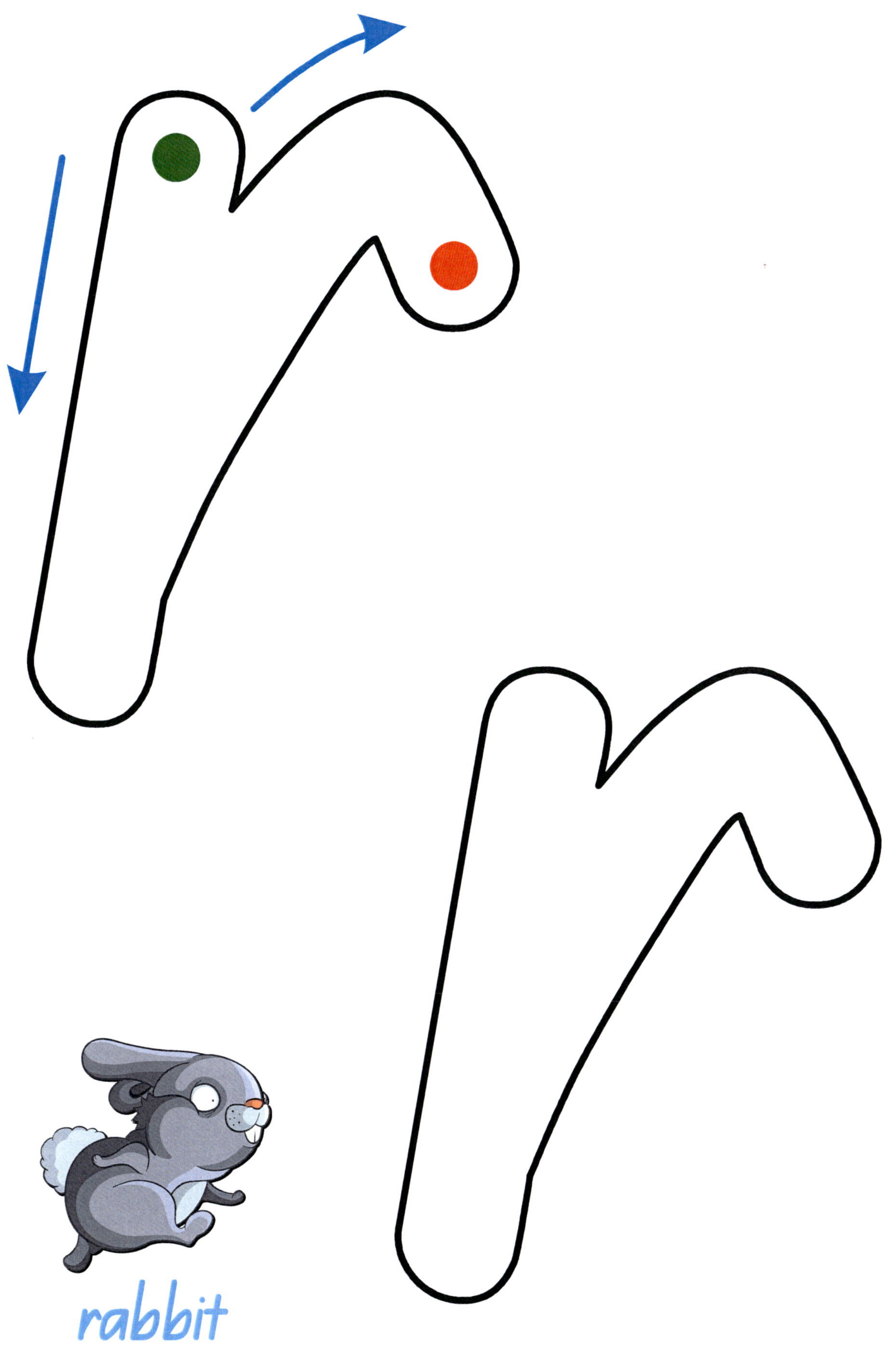
rabbit

ball

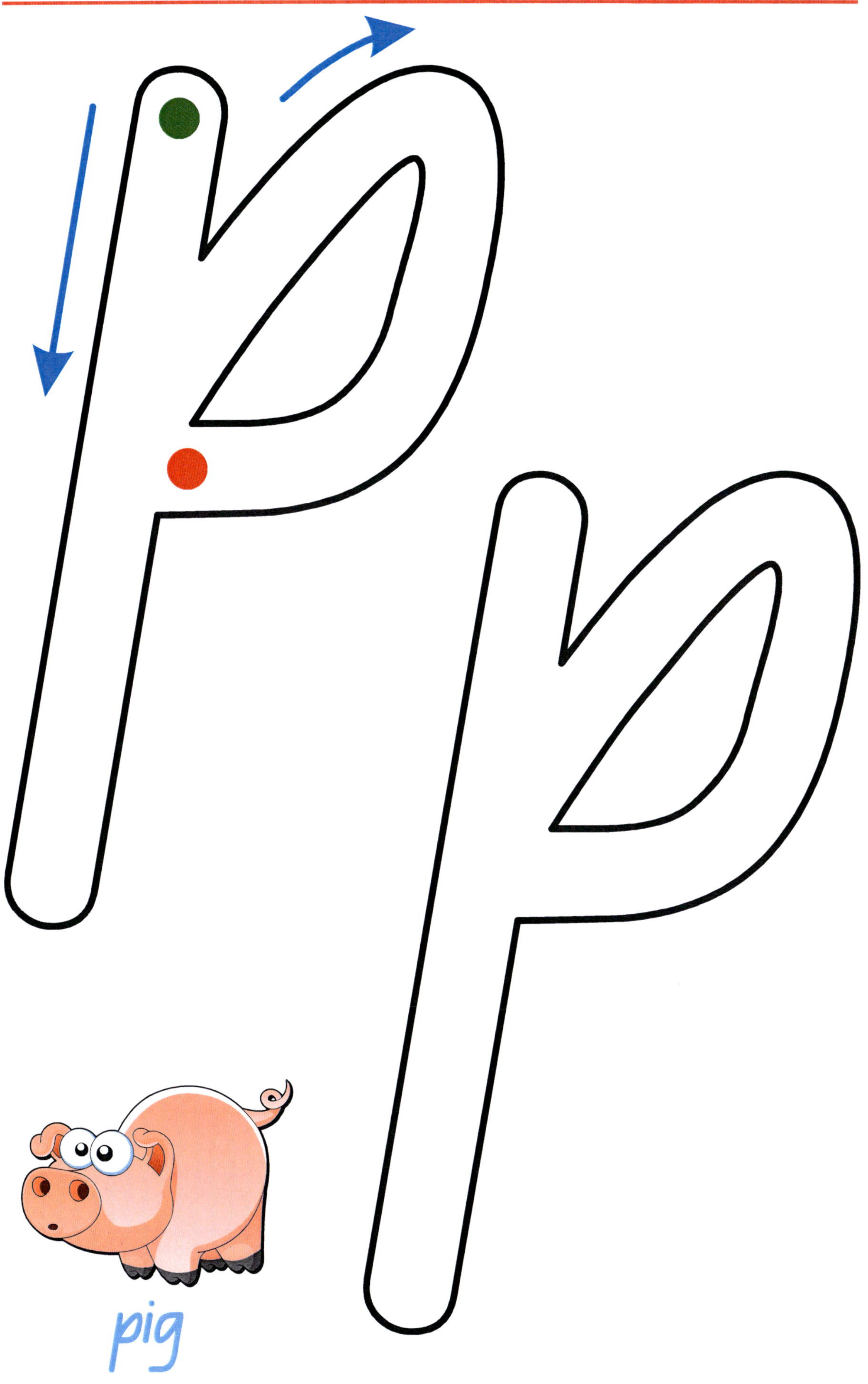
pig

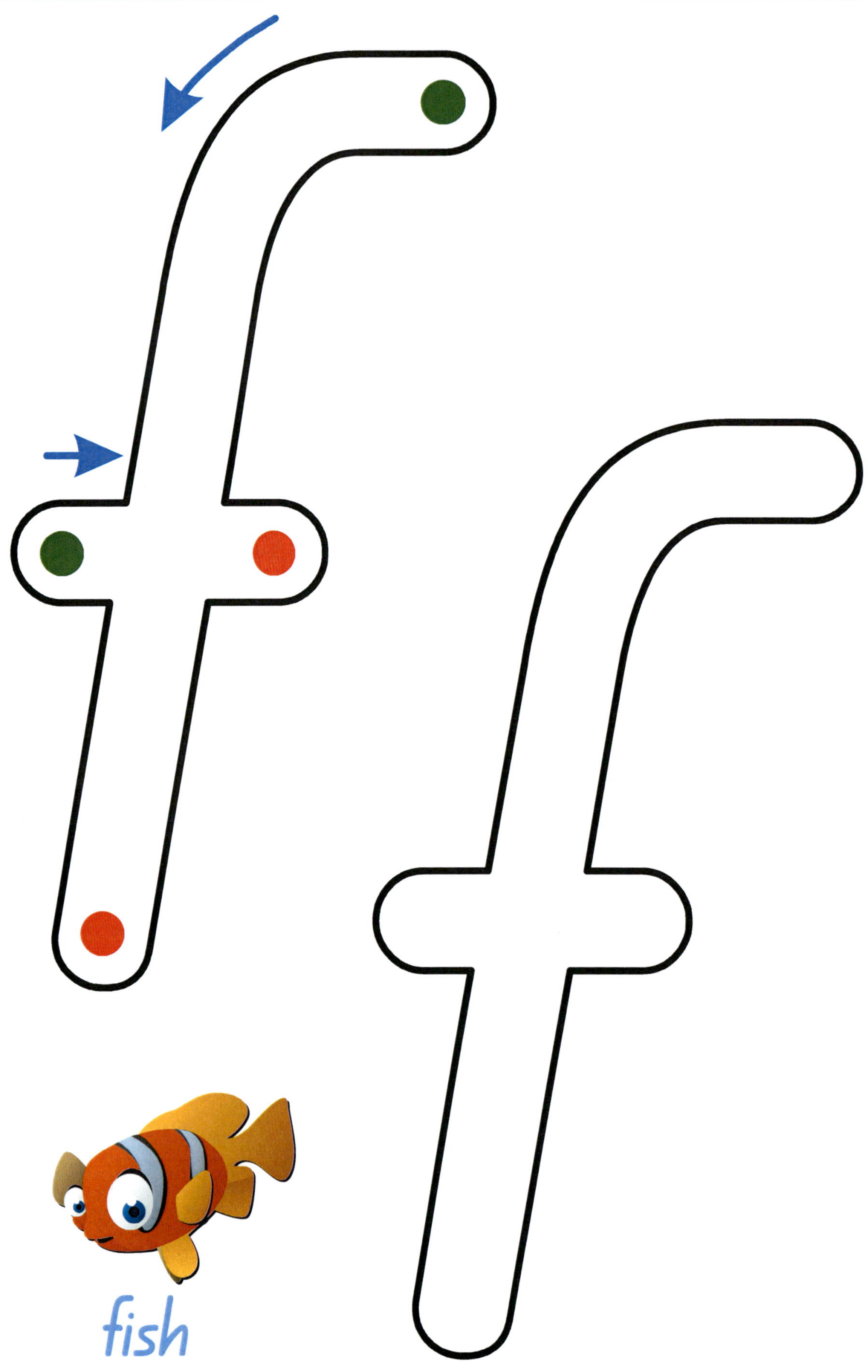
fish

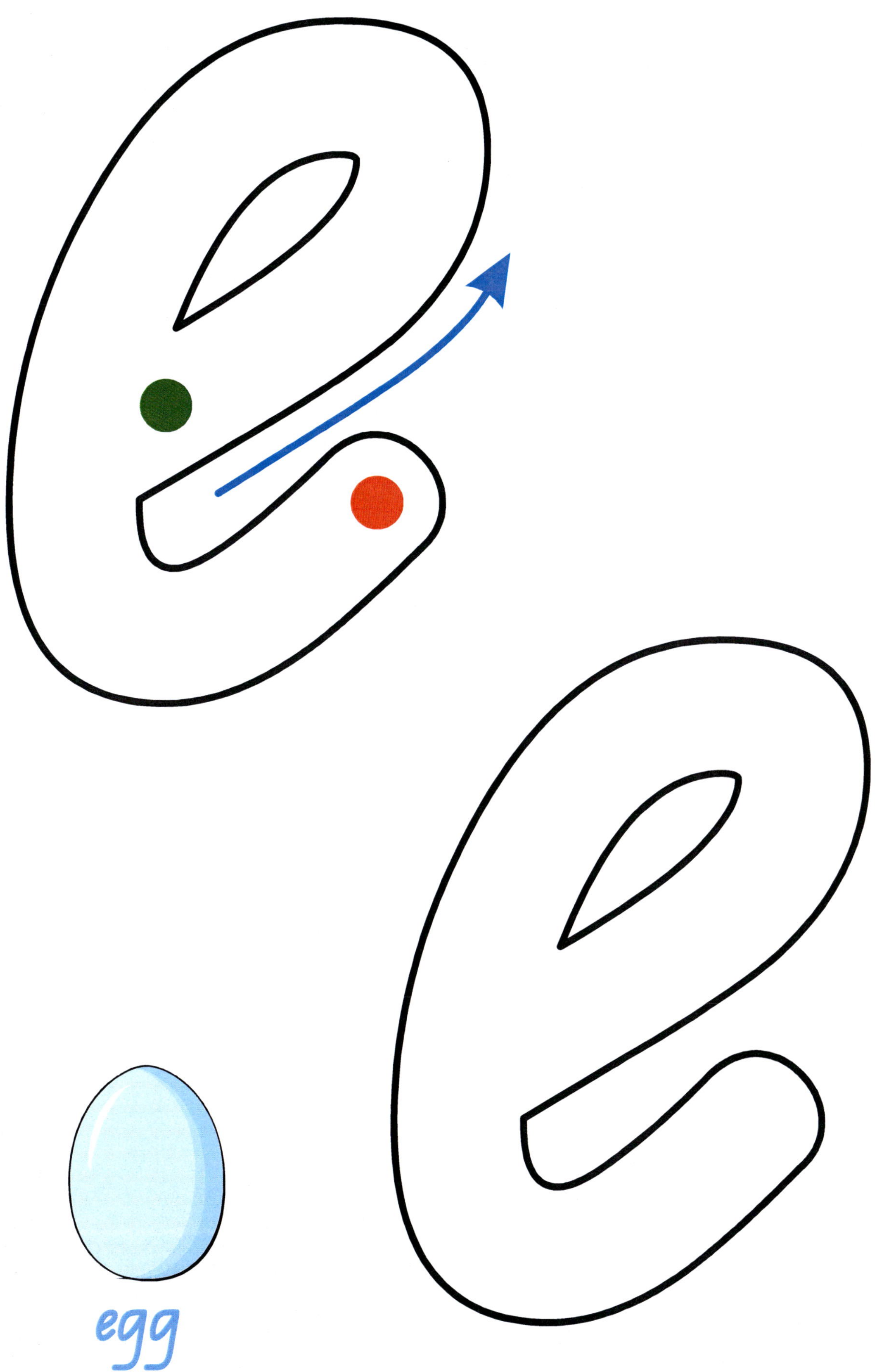

egg

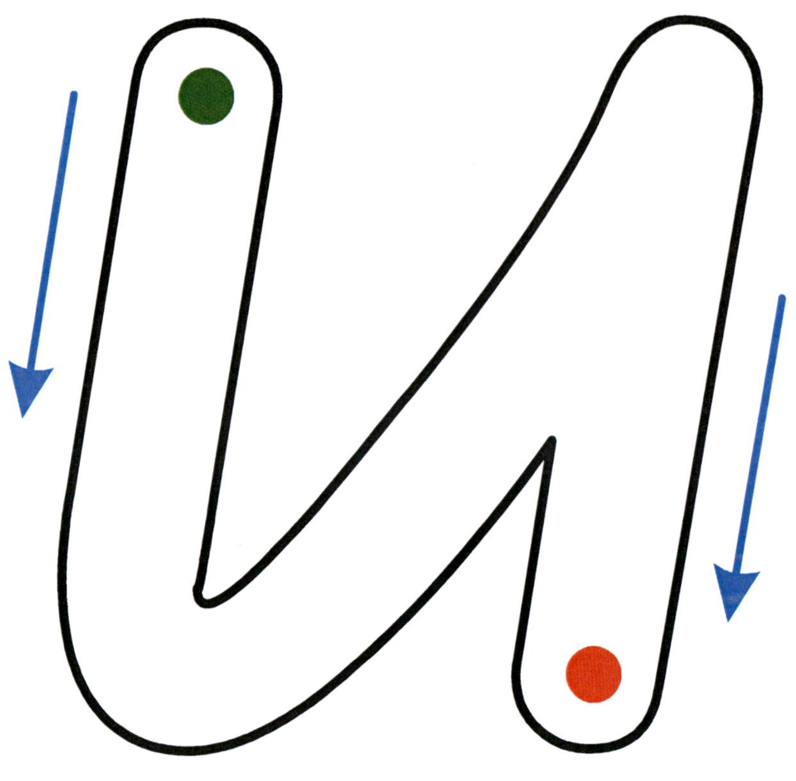

umbrella

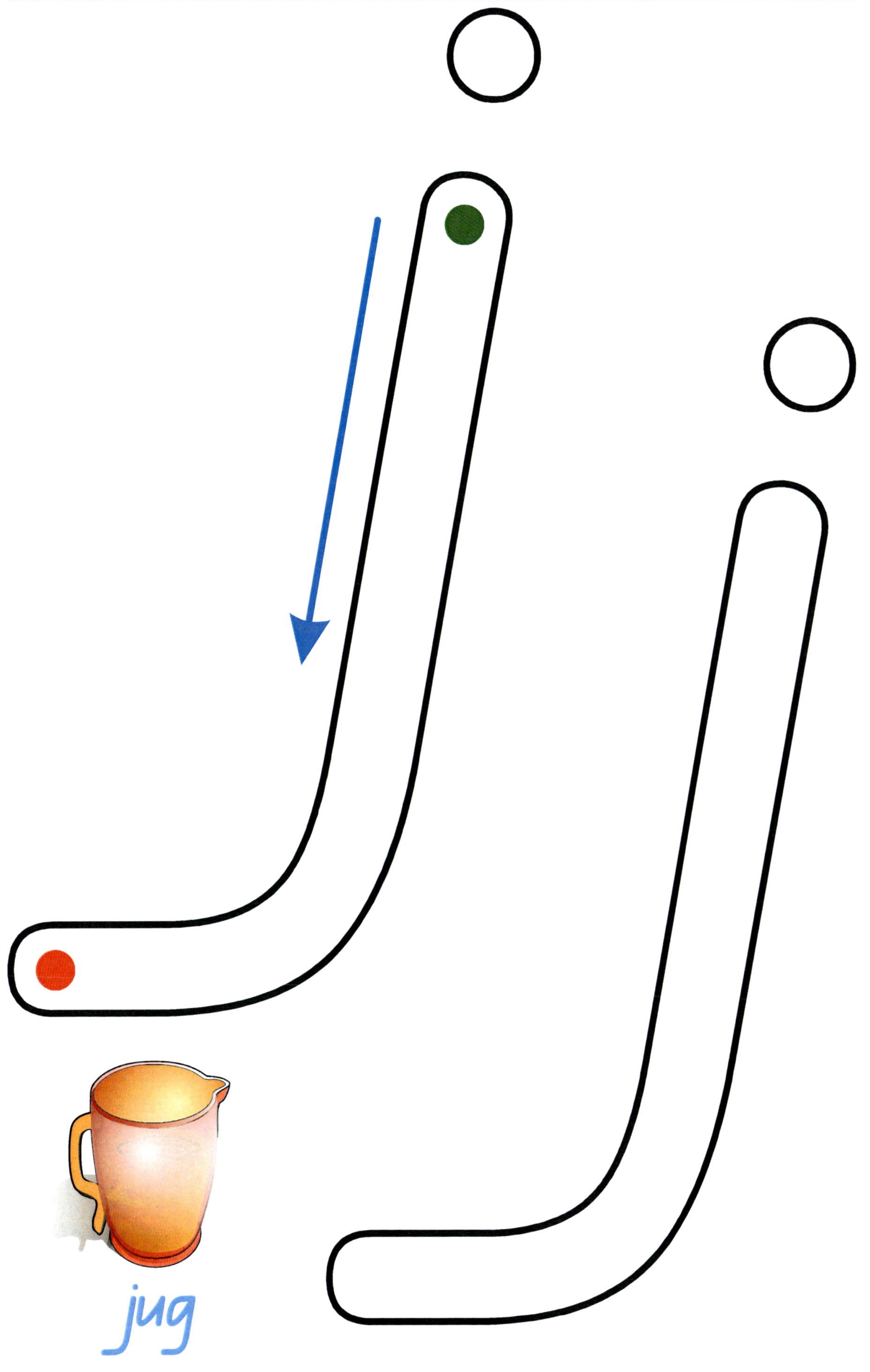
jug

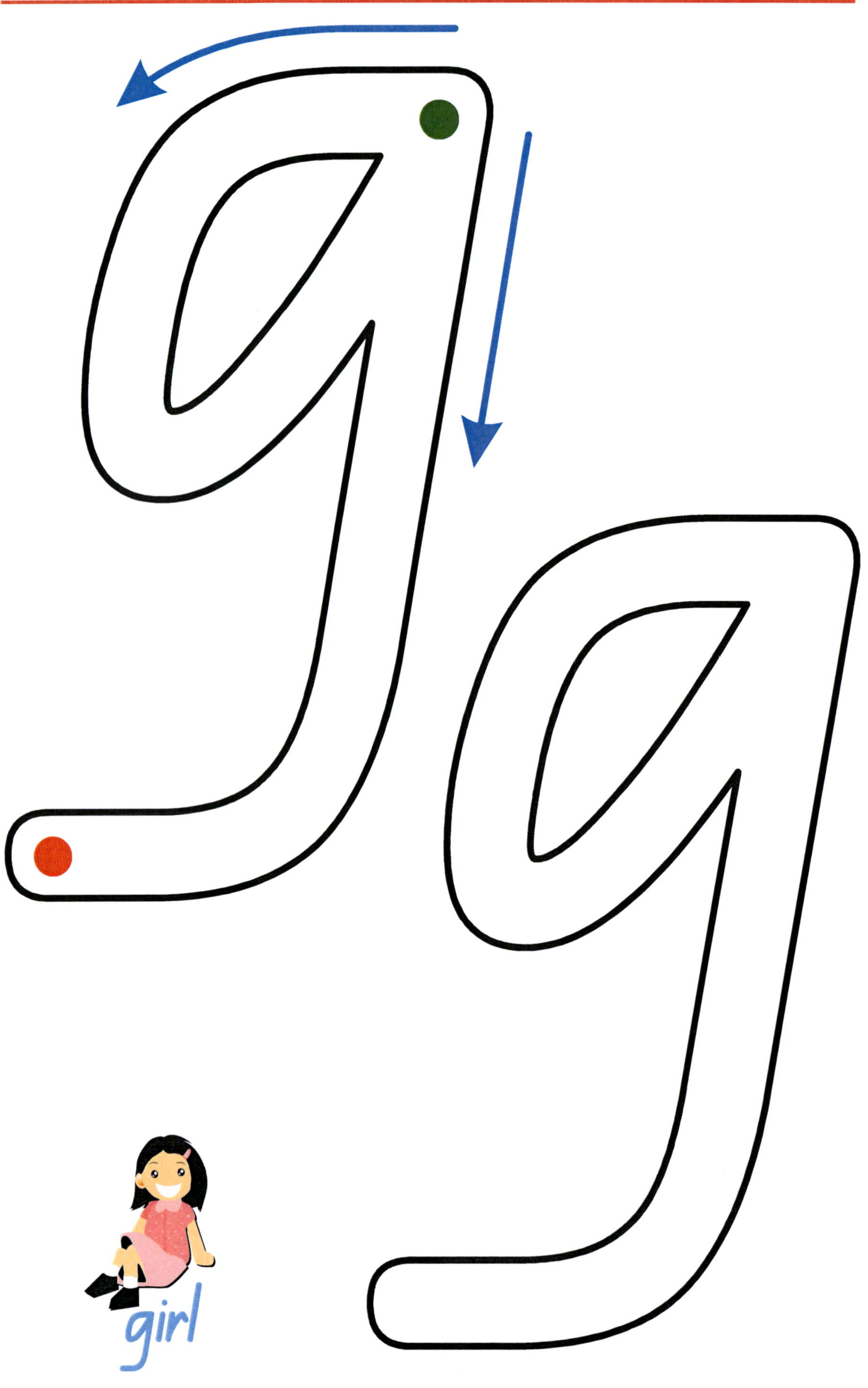
girl

queen

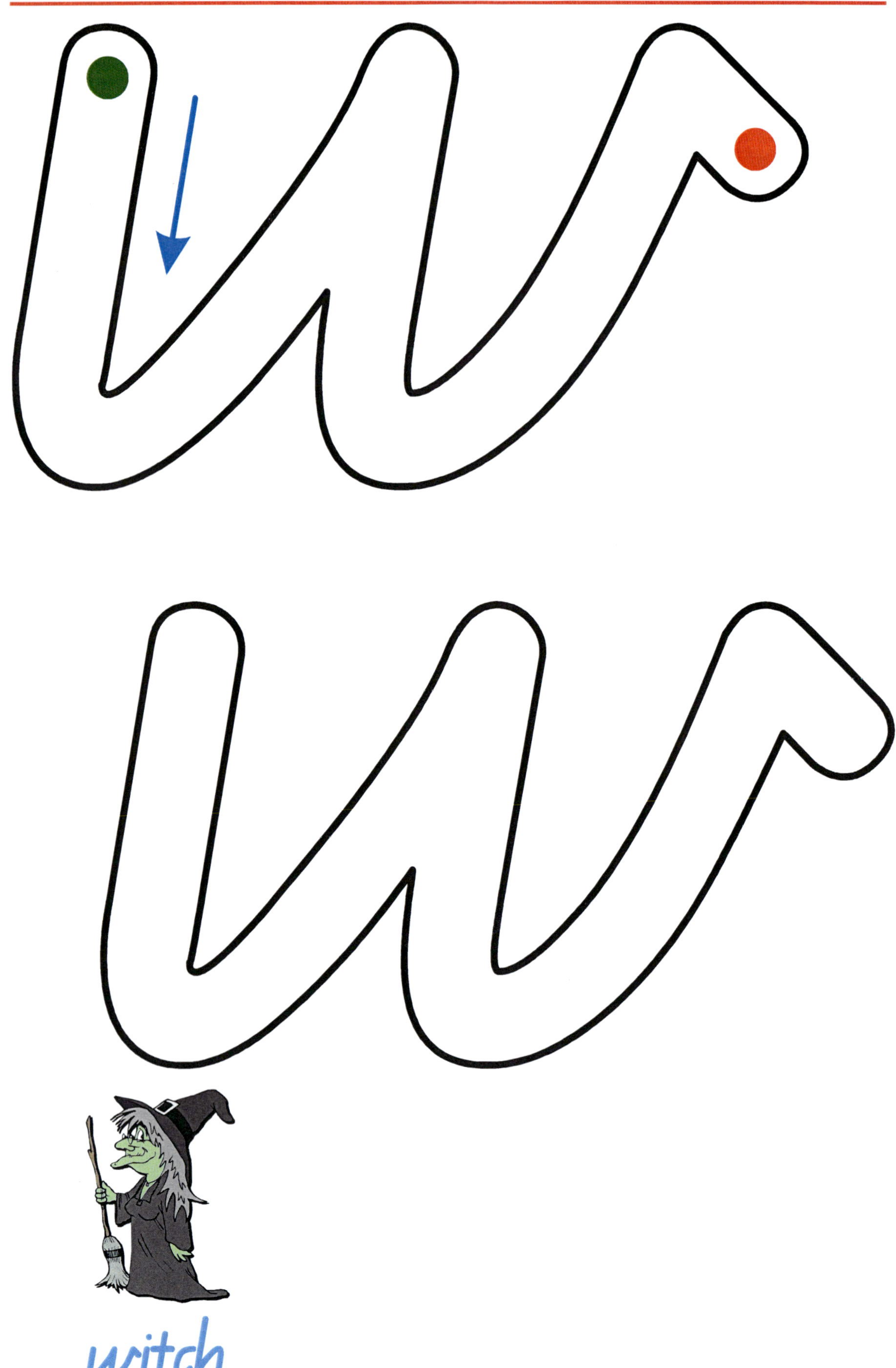

witch

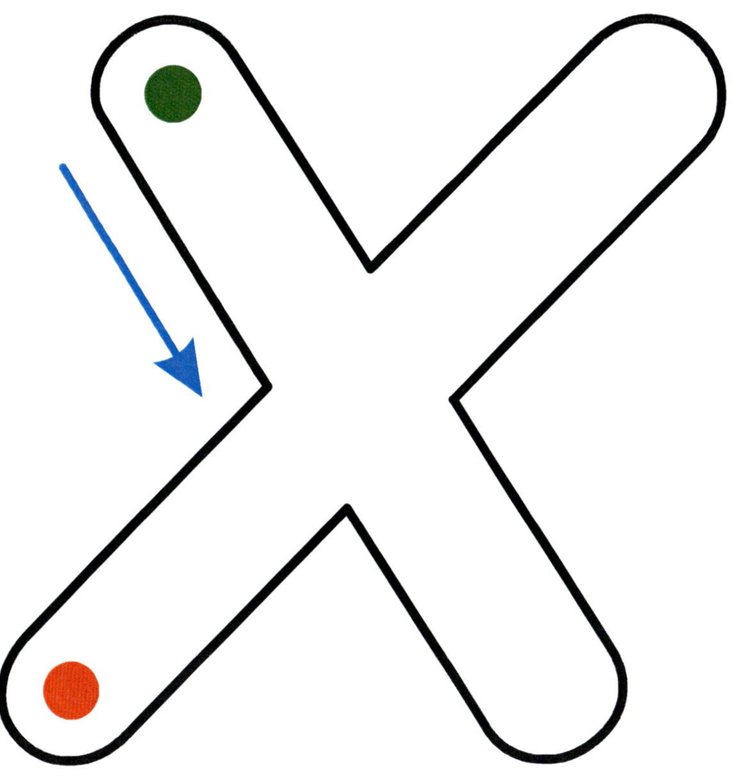

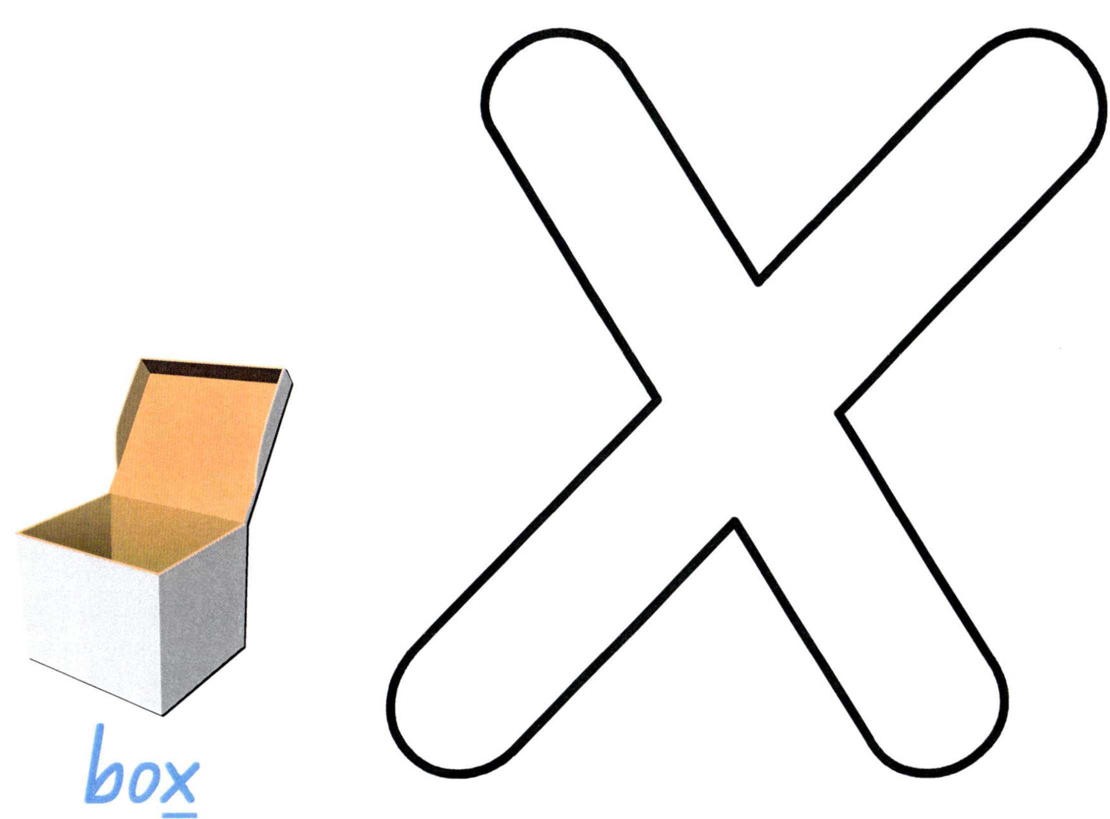
box

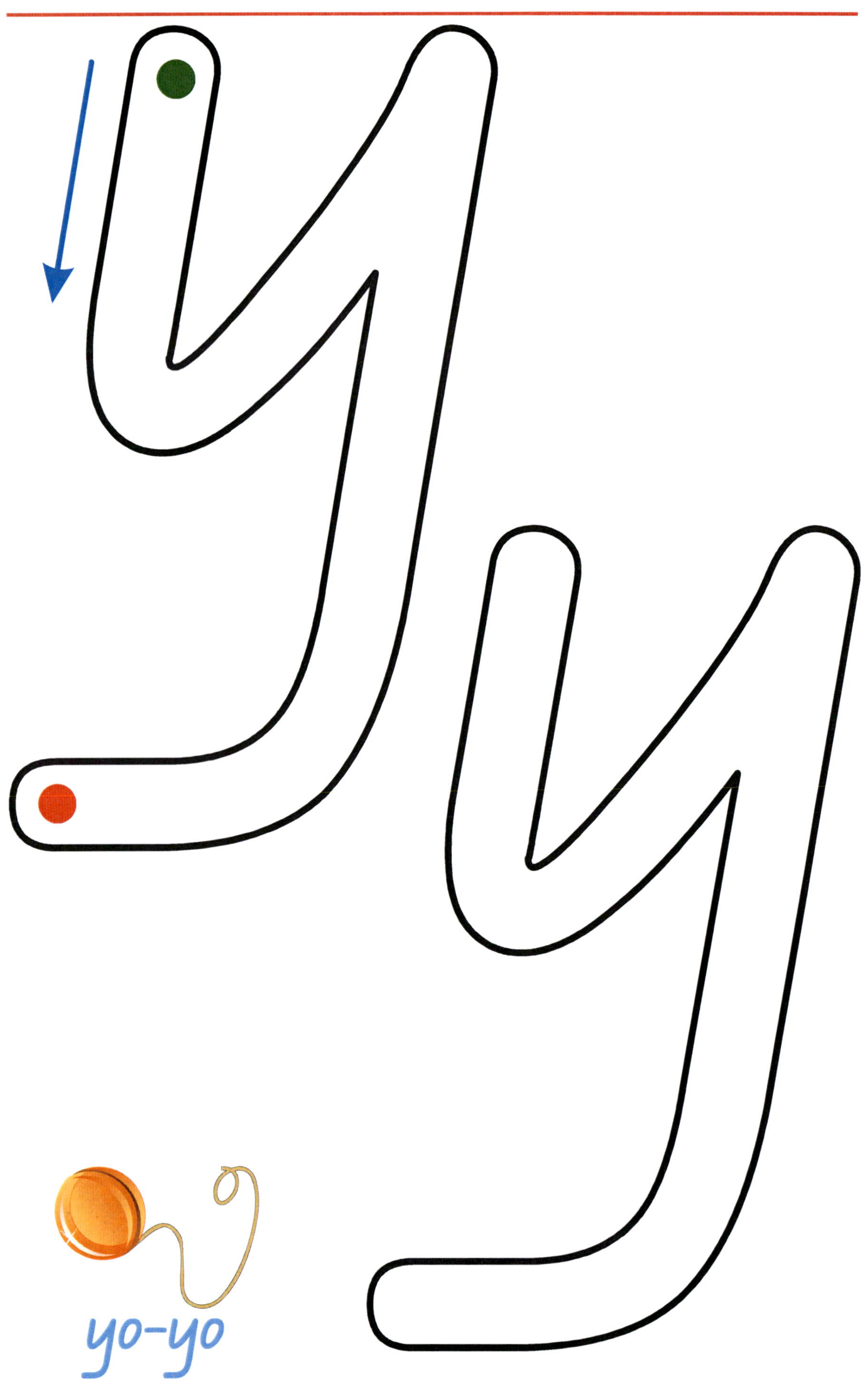
yo-yo

sun

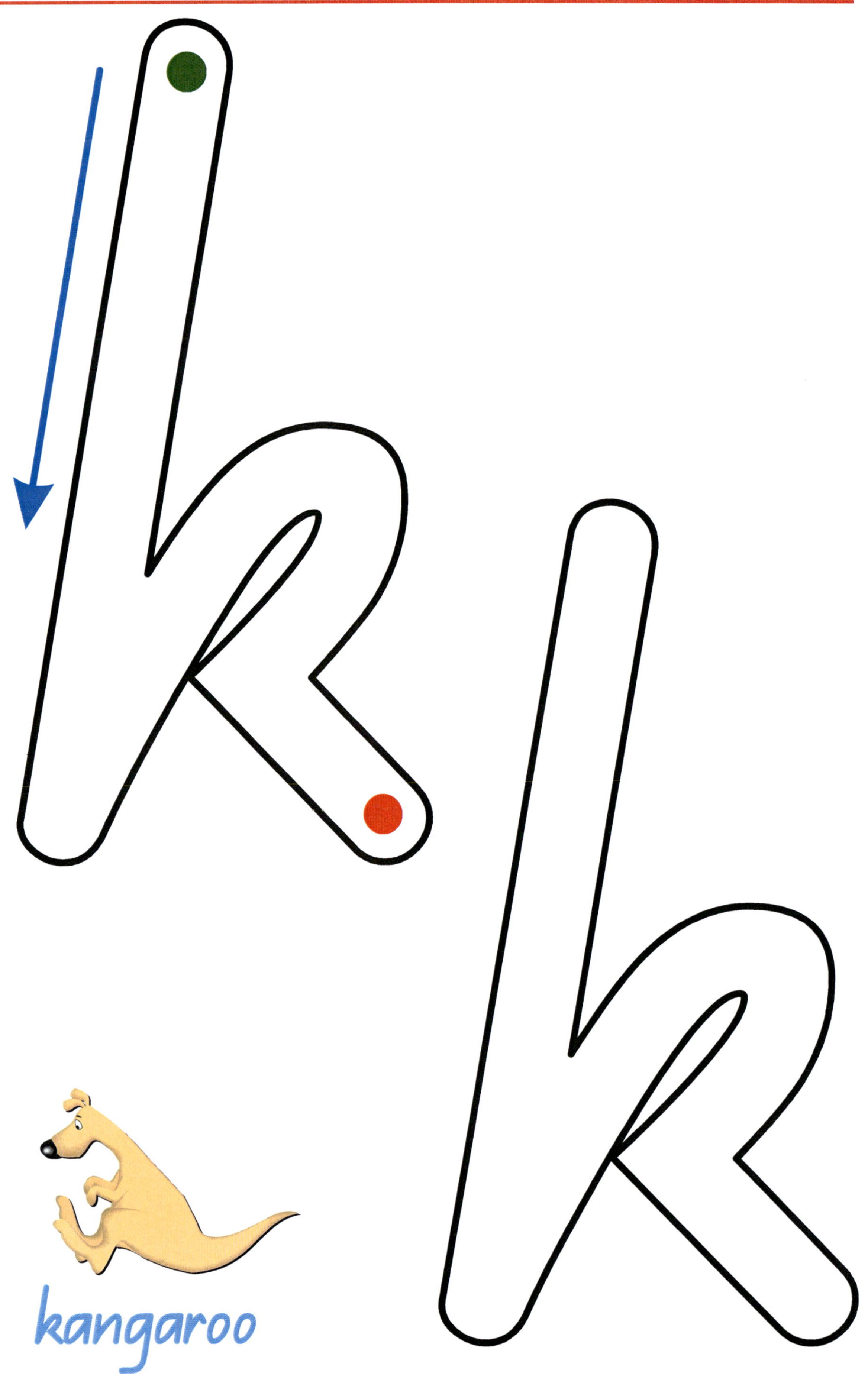
kangaroo

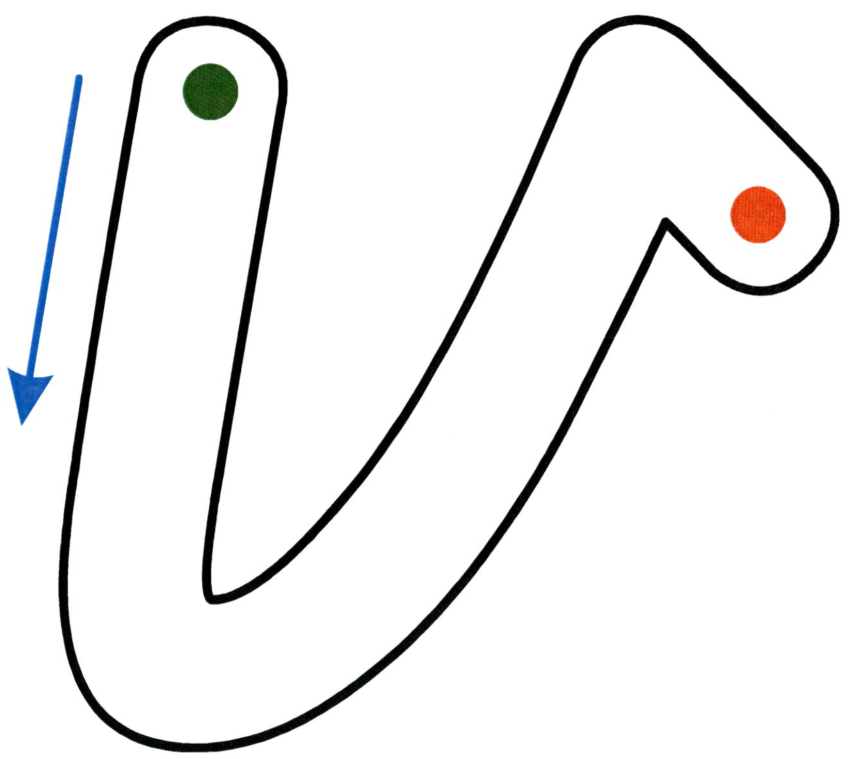

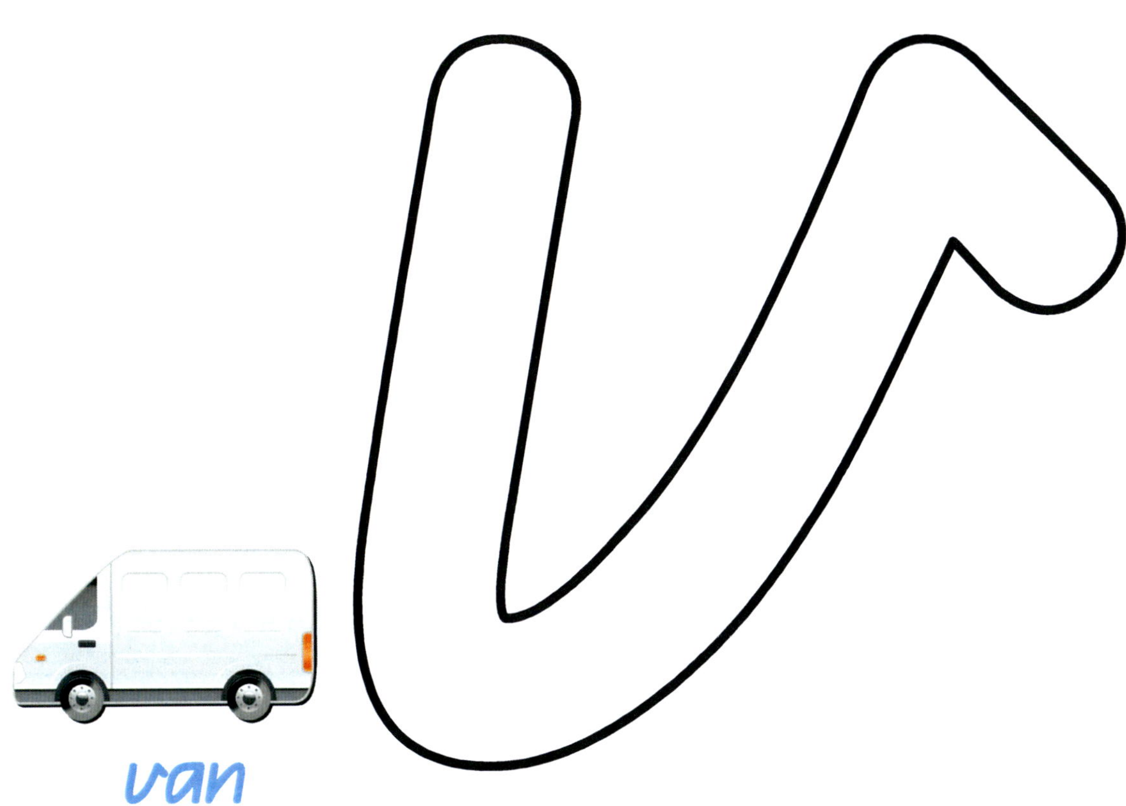
van

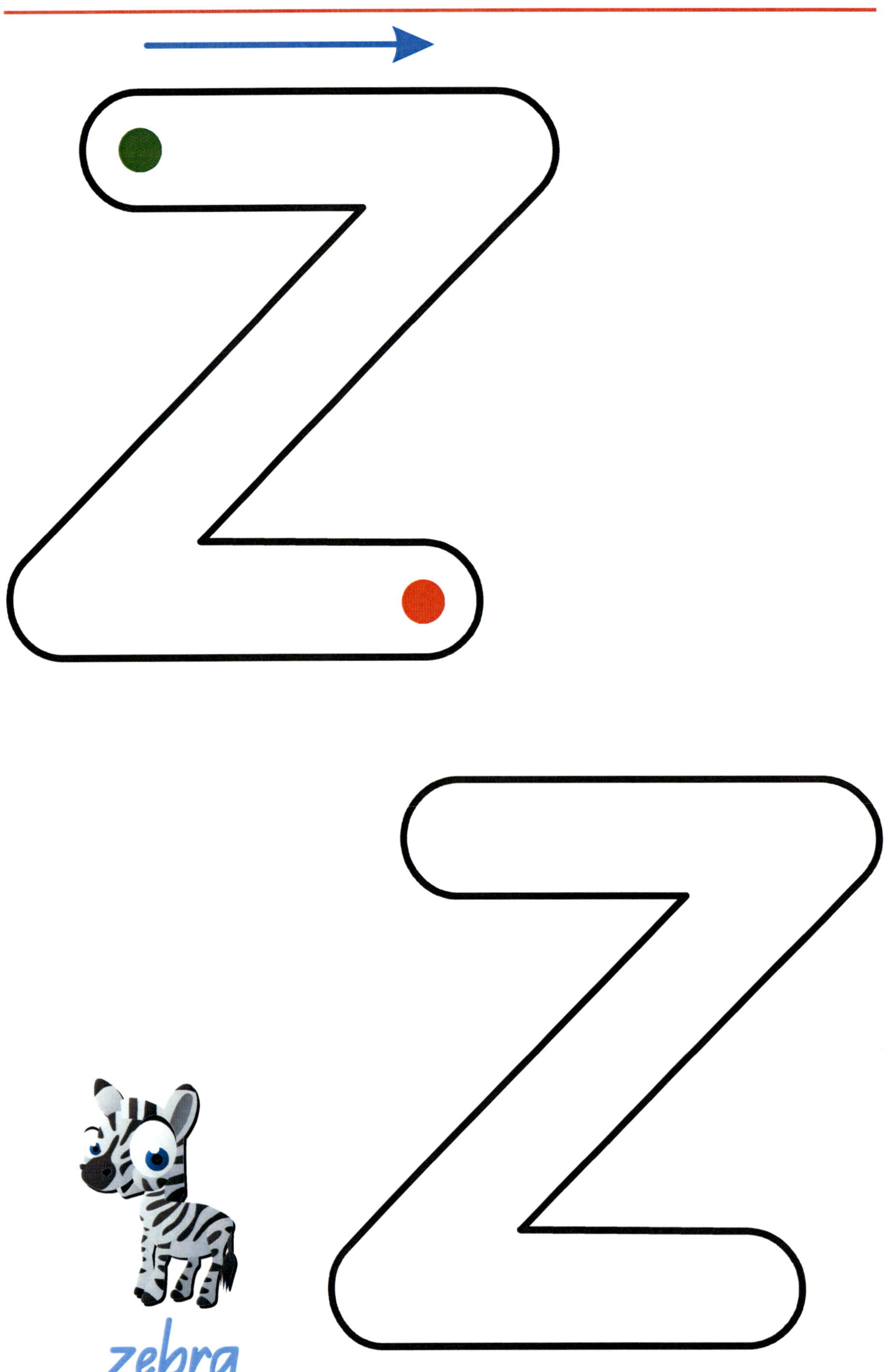
zebra

HANDWRITING LINK

Letters on a Single Line

Blank page intentionally added.

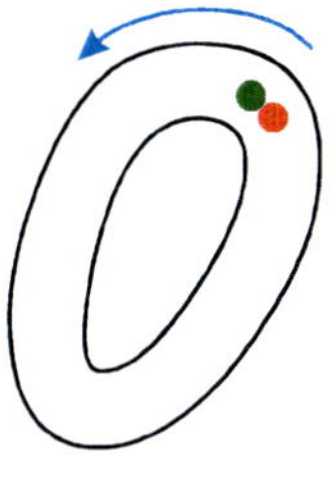

o

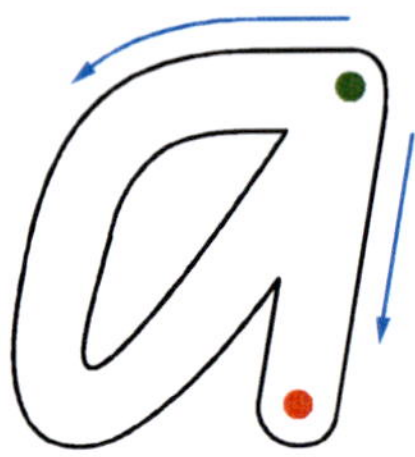

a

c

i

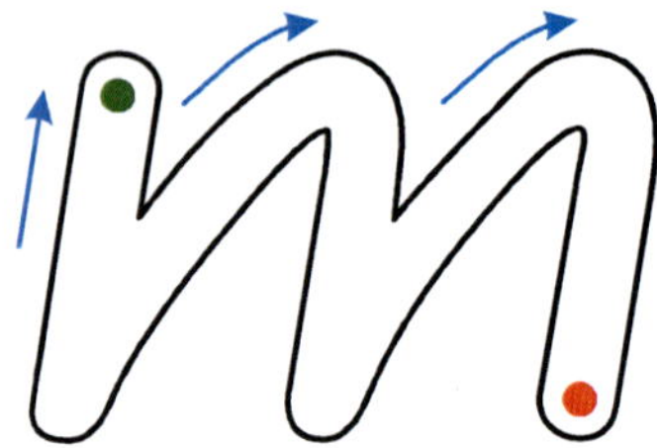

m

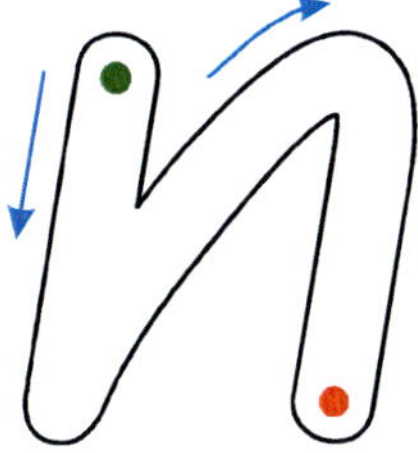

n

r

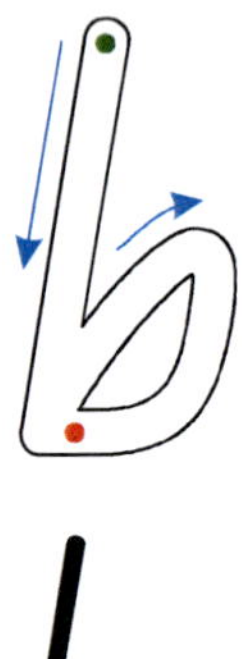

b

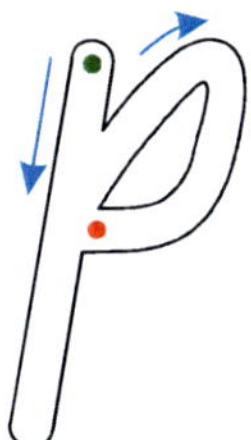

p

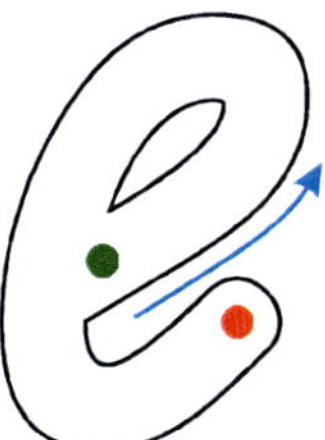

e

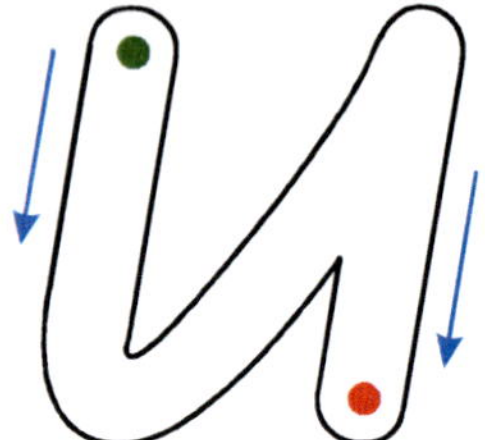

и

j

j

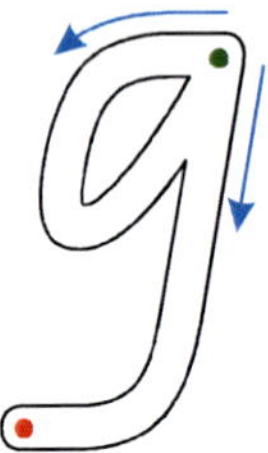

g

qu

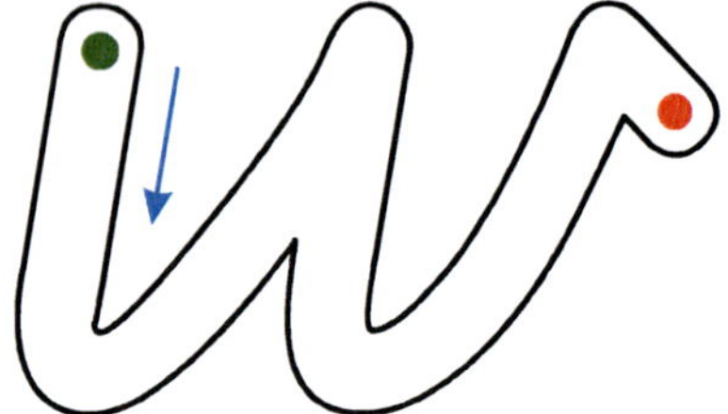

w

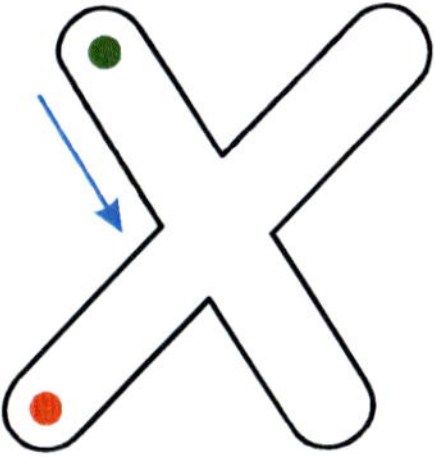

x

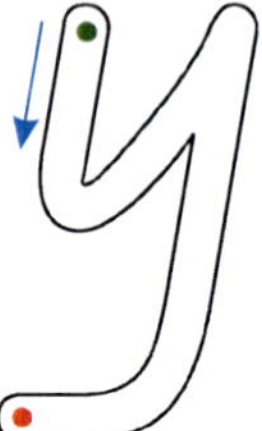

y

s

k

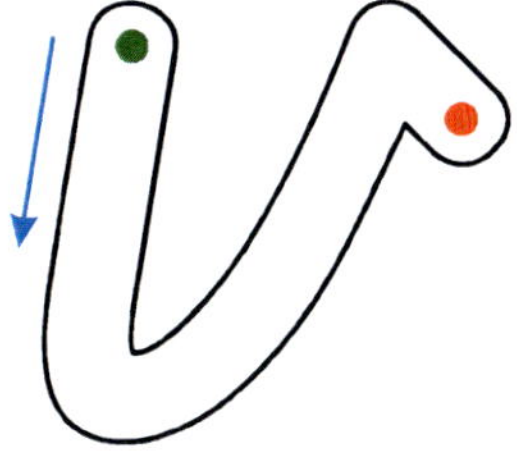

v

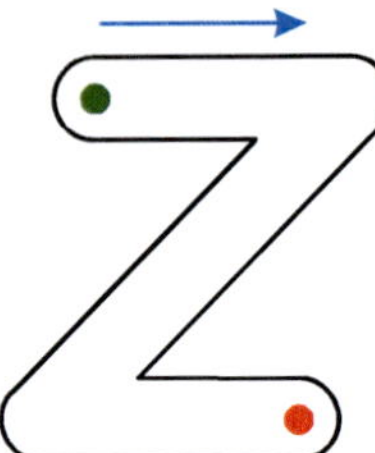

z

Multiple Letters on a Single Line

Blank page intentionally added.

o

a

ao

oa

d

da

do

ad

od

c

ca

co

ac

oc

i

ia

ai

io

did

l

li

ill

call

doll

t

it

to

at

cat

dot

m

ma

om

mill

mat

n

ni

on

nod

tin

h

hi

oh

him

had

r

or

ran

rim

car

b

bo

bat

rob

bit

p

ip

pan

pot

lip

f

fi

off

fin

fan

e

ei

ae

fed

hen

u

mu

ur

fun

mud

g

gr

ig

egg

fig

grub

j

je

jog

jam

jet

qu

que

qui

quell

queen

quoll

w

we

ew

wag

web

with

x

ex

axe

fox

box

y

ye

ey

yell

yum

play

s

se

six

hiss

mess

send

k

ke

kick

luck

peck

v

ev

van

vet

vest

vote

z

zinc

zoo

zipper

zoom

zigzag

Introducing Capitals

Blank page intentionally added.

oO

o

O

Oo

a A

a

A

Aa

Ao

dD

d

D

Dd

da

Da

Do

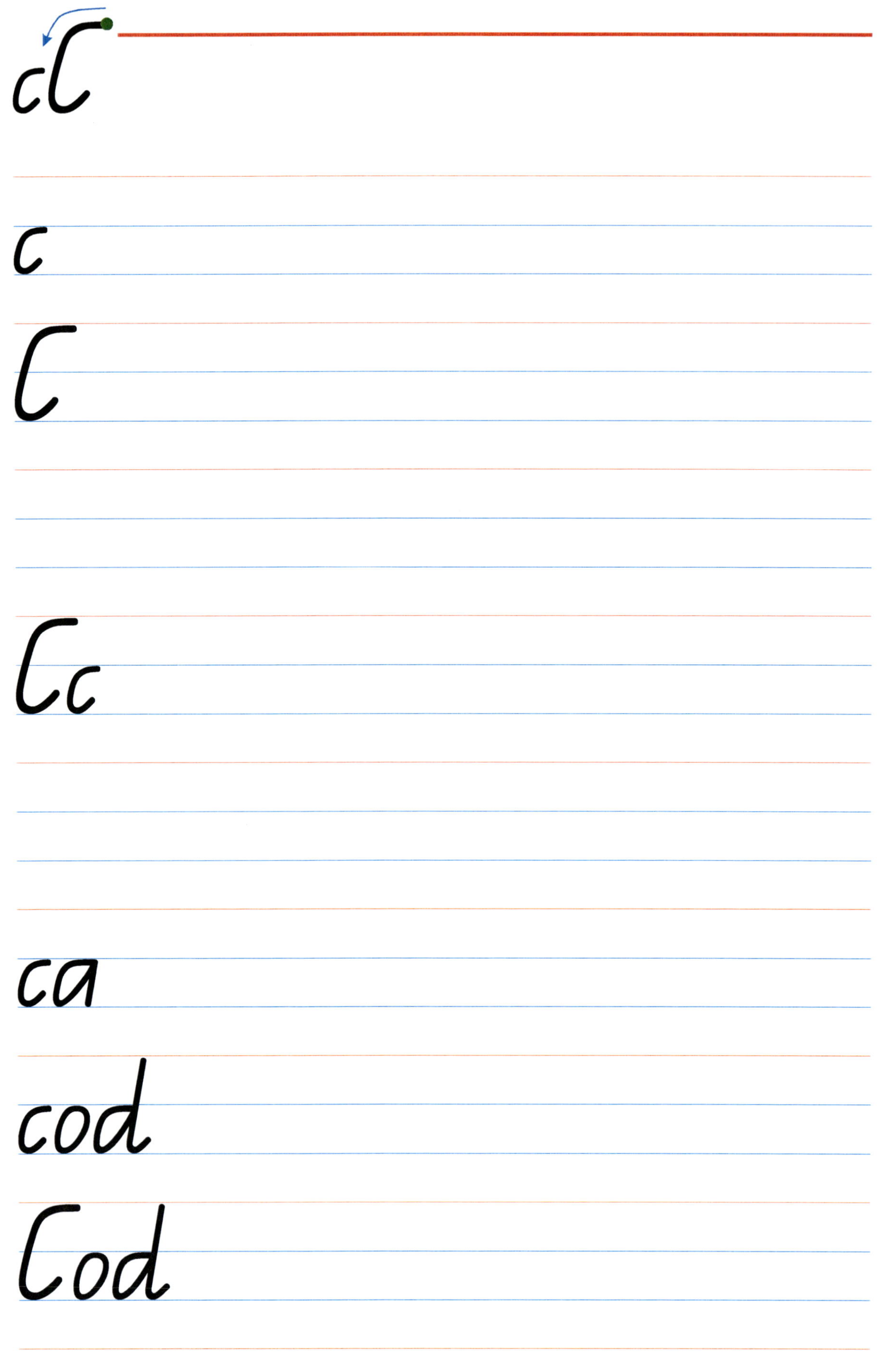
cC
c
C
Cc
ca
cod
Cod

iI

i

I

iI

Ia

Io

did

Ll
l
L
Ll
Ill
Lid
Call

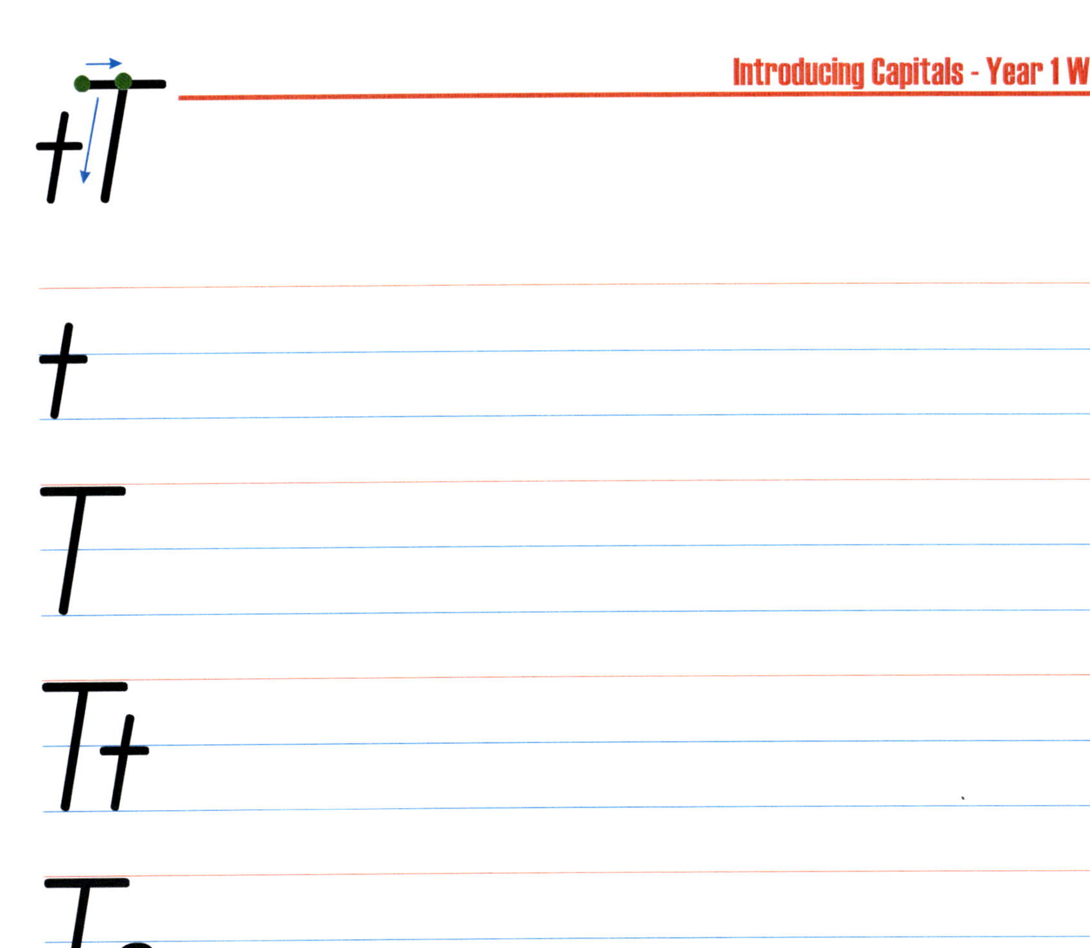

tT

t

T

Tt

To

Dot

Lot

Lit

cot

mM

m

M

Mm

Mat

Tim

Mill

am

Mat

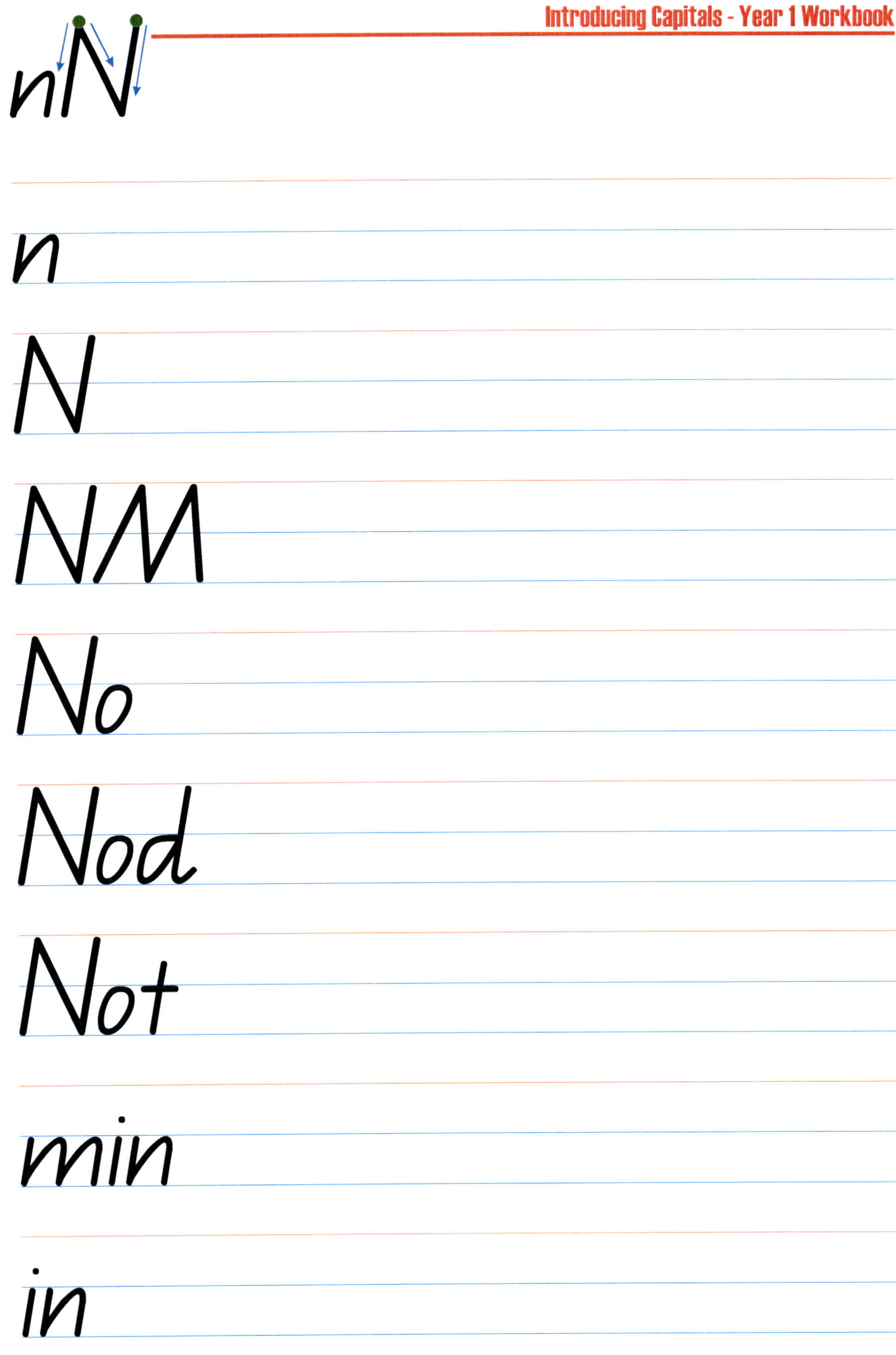
nN
n
N
NM
No
Nod
Not
min
in

hH
h
H
Hh
Hat
Hot
Him
Hall
hill

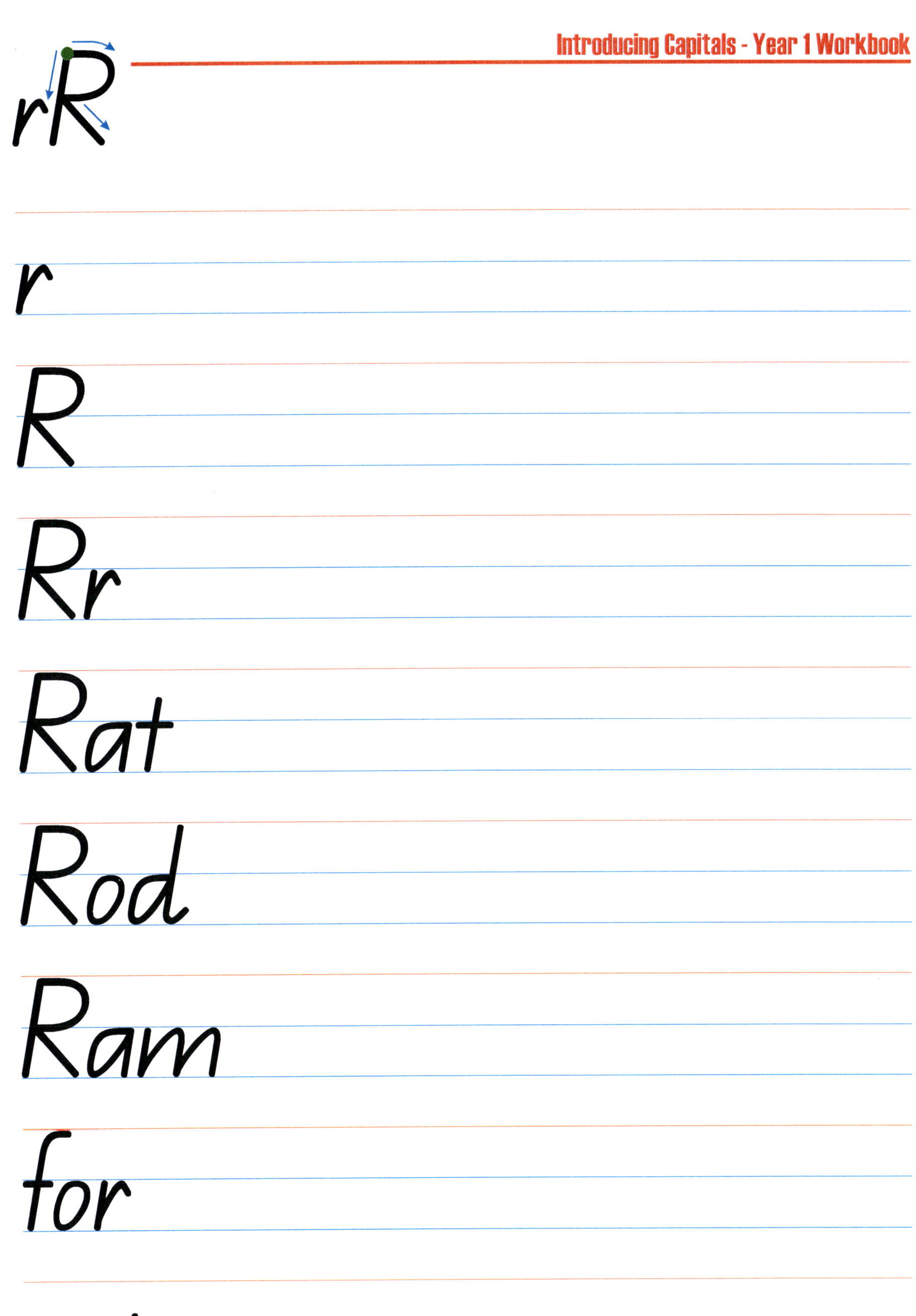
rR
r
R
Rr
Rat
Rod
Ram
for
grin

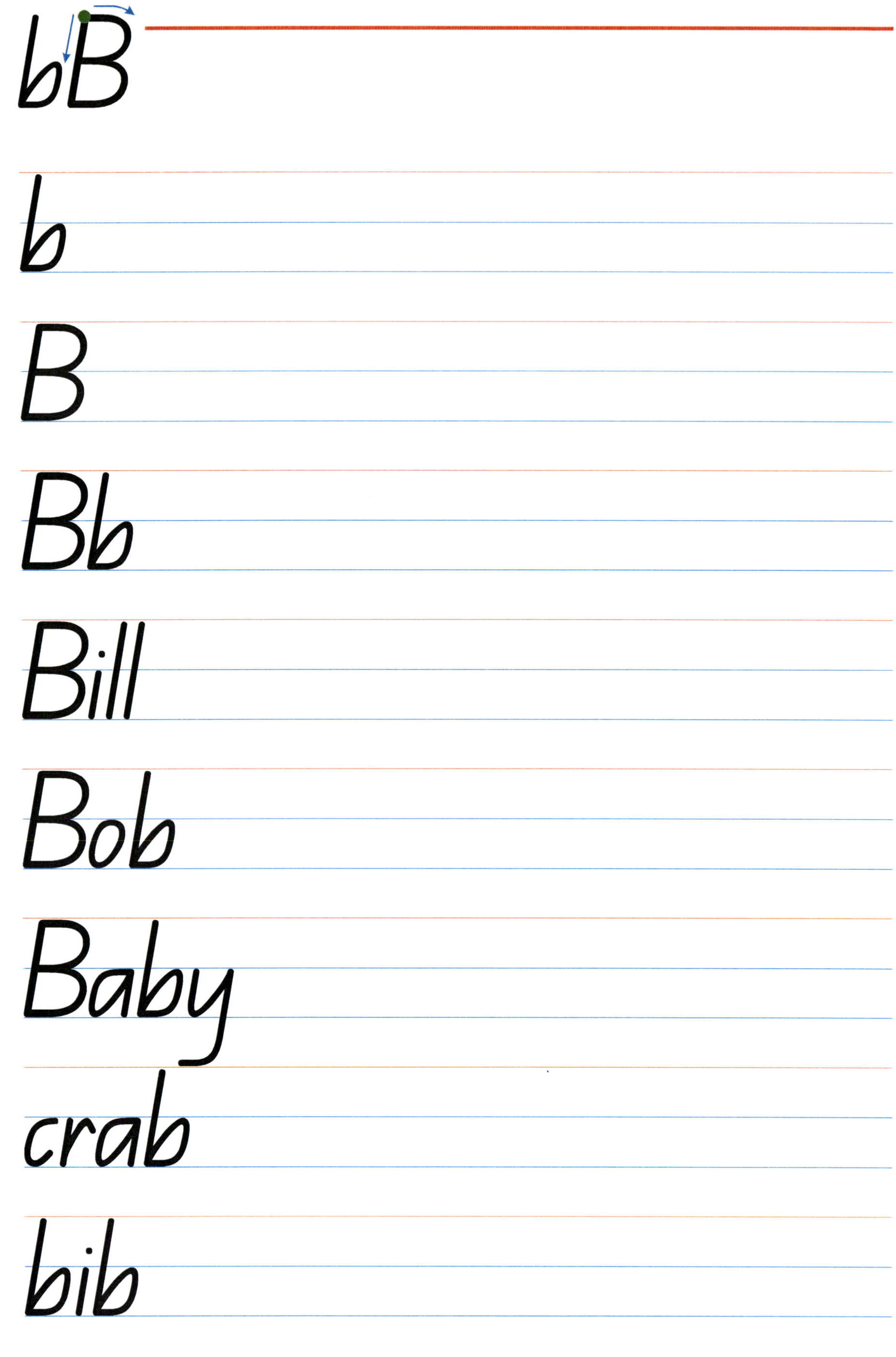
bB
b
B
Bb
Bill
Bob
Baby
crab
bib

pP

p

P

Pp

Pat

Pan

Pin

Plan

clap

fF
f
F
Ff
Fran
Flag
frog
fig
from

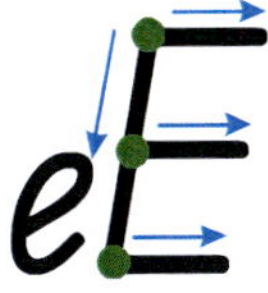

e

E

Ee

Egg

Eel

Elf

men

pen

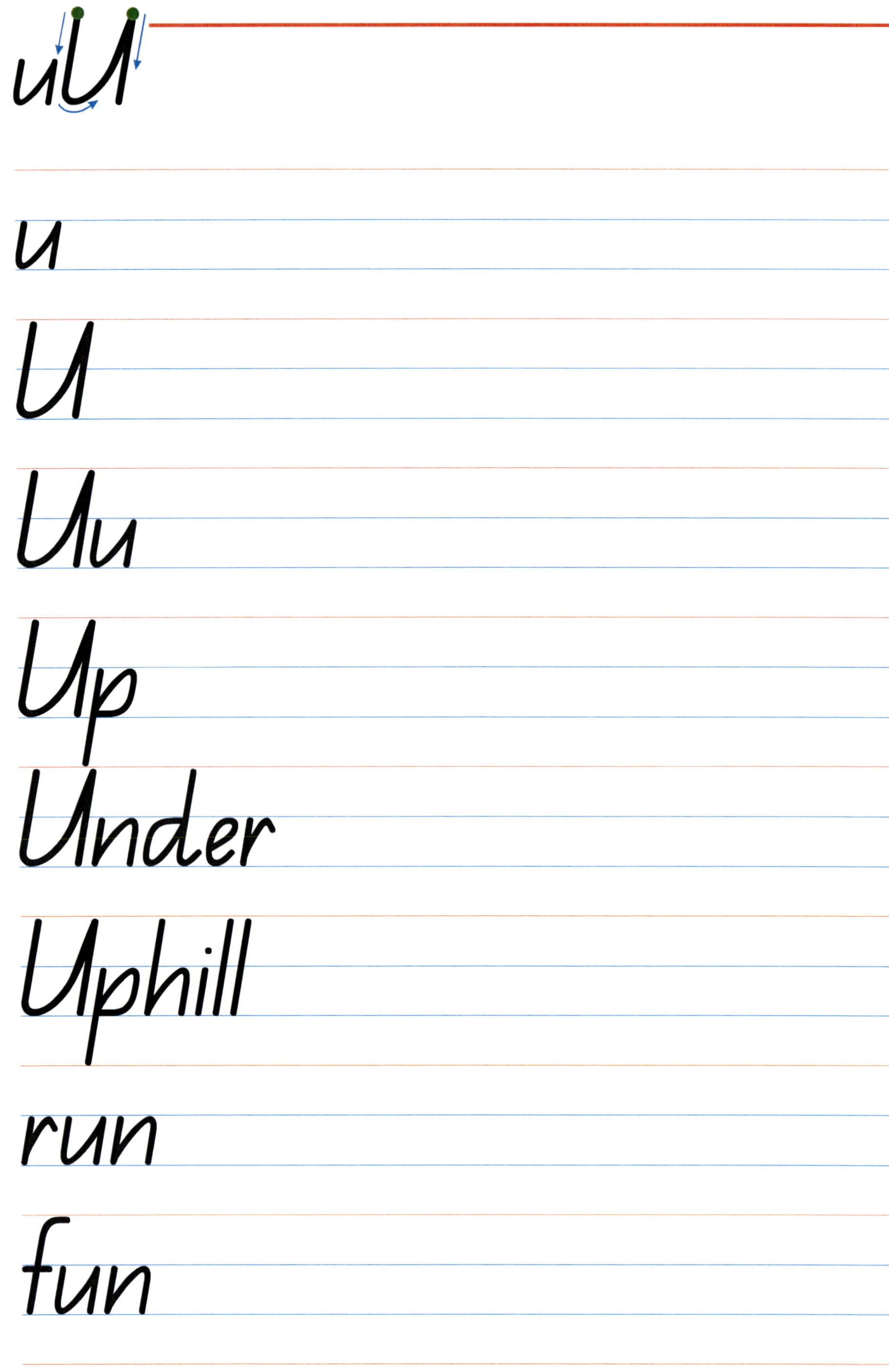
uU
u
U
Uu
Up
Under
Uphill
run
fun

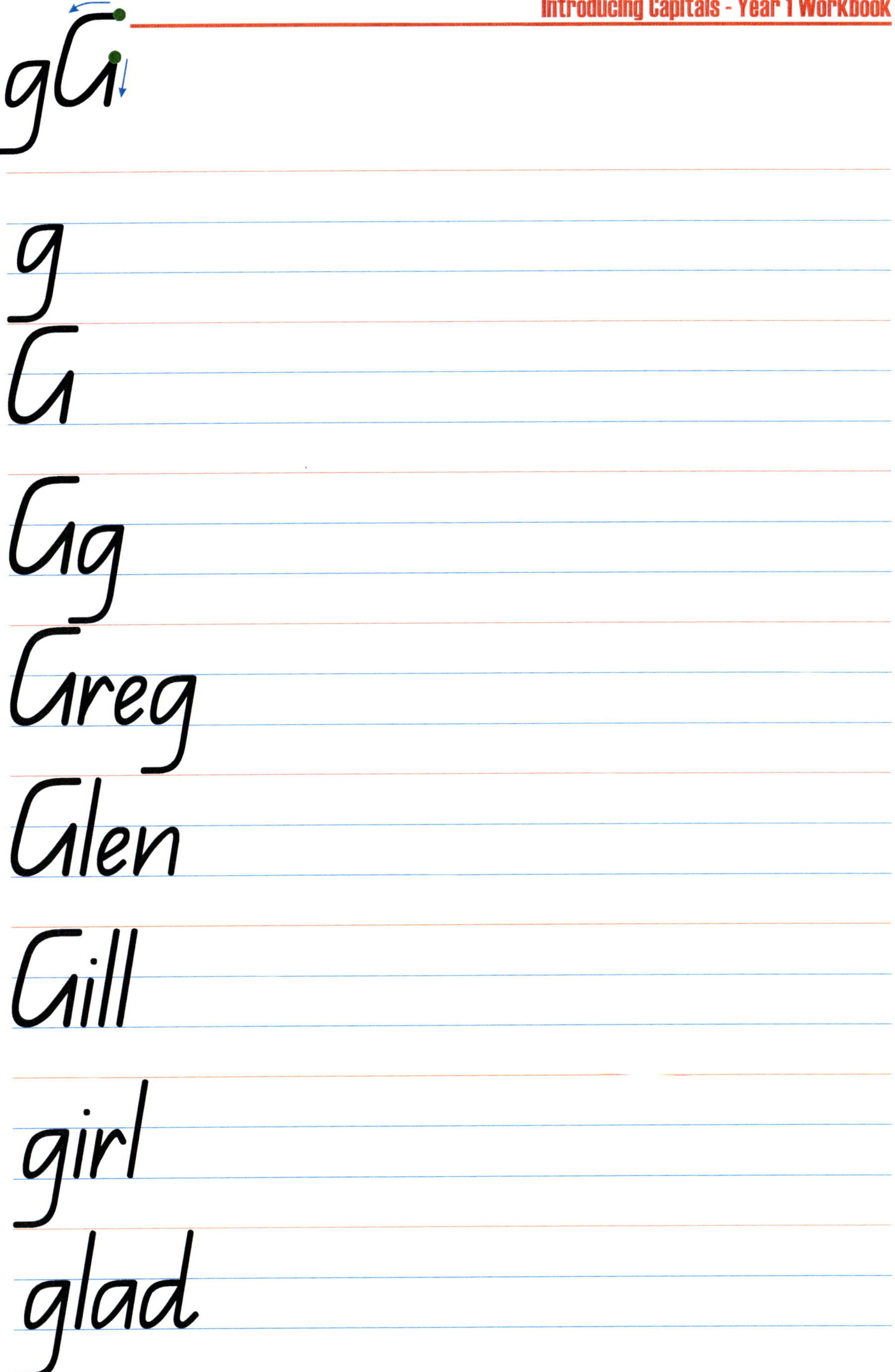
gG
g
G
Gg
Greg
Glen
Gill
girl
glad

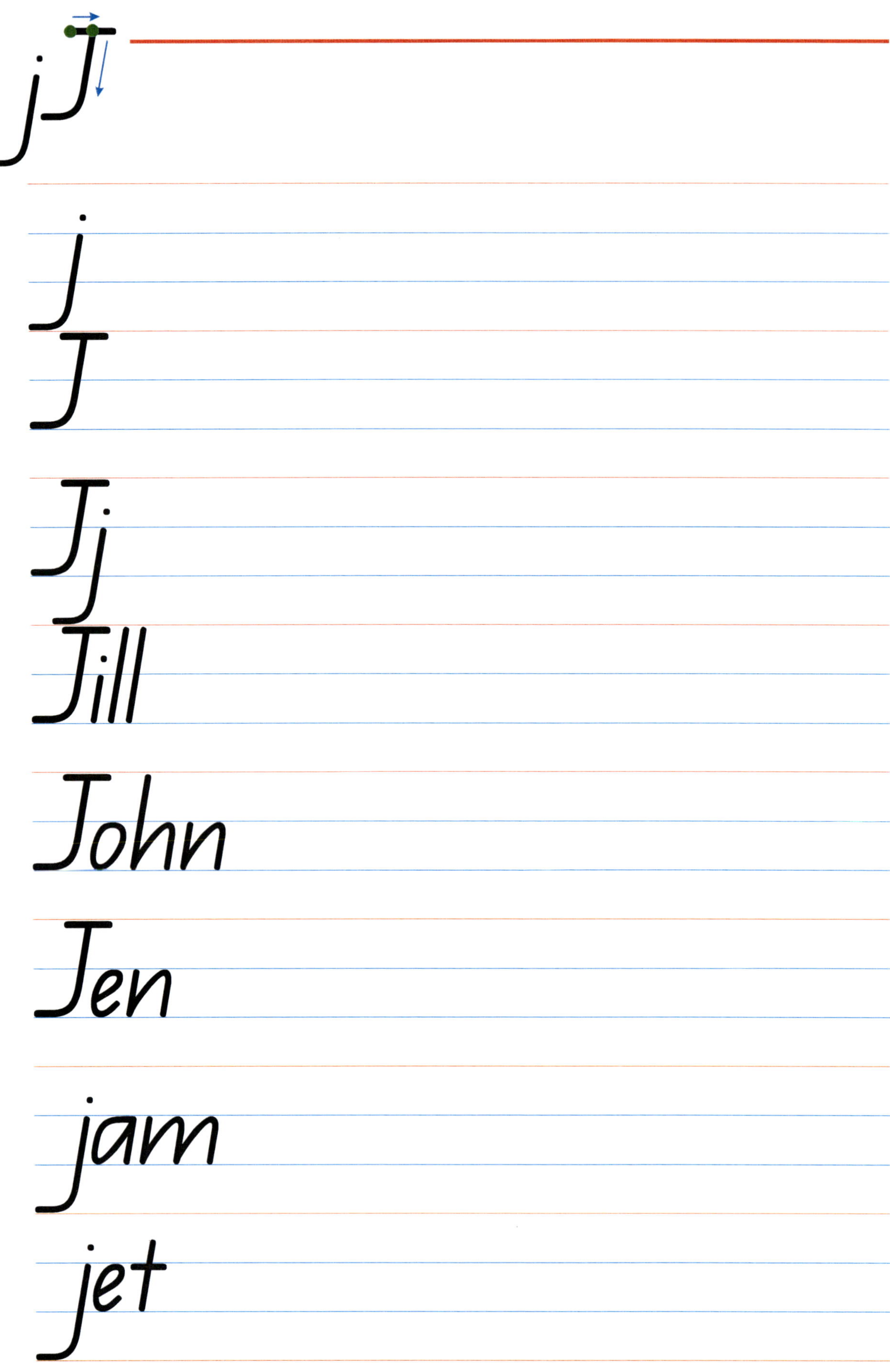

j J
j
J
Jj
Jill
John
Jen
jam
jet

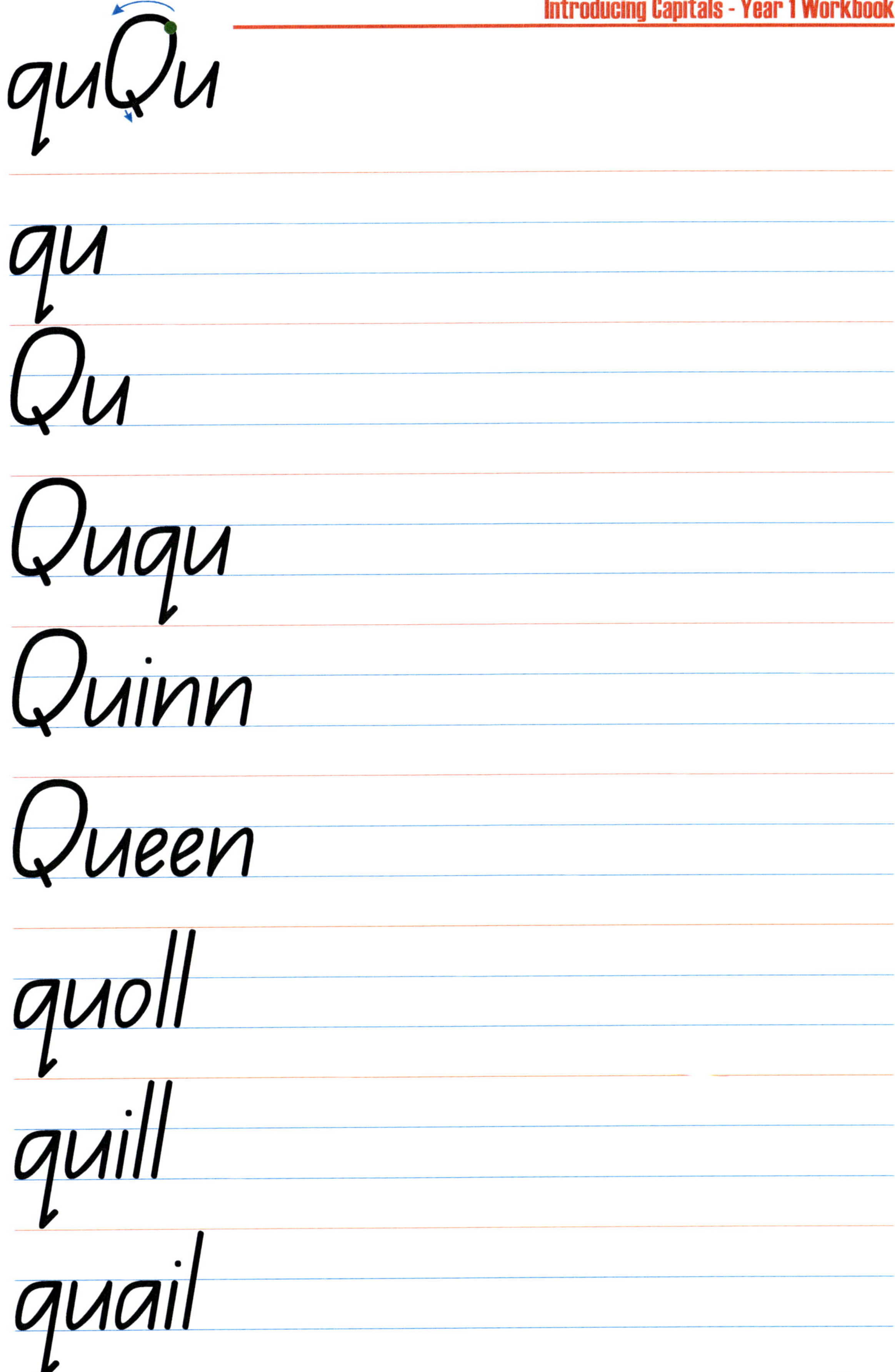
quQu
qu
Qu
Ququ
Quinn
Queen
quoll
quill
quail

wW

w

W

Ww

Walt

William

web

wind

wing

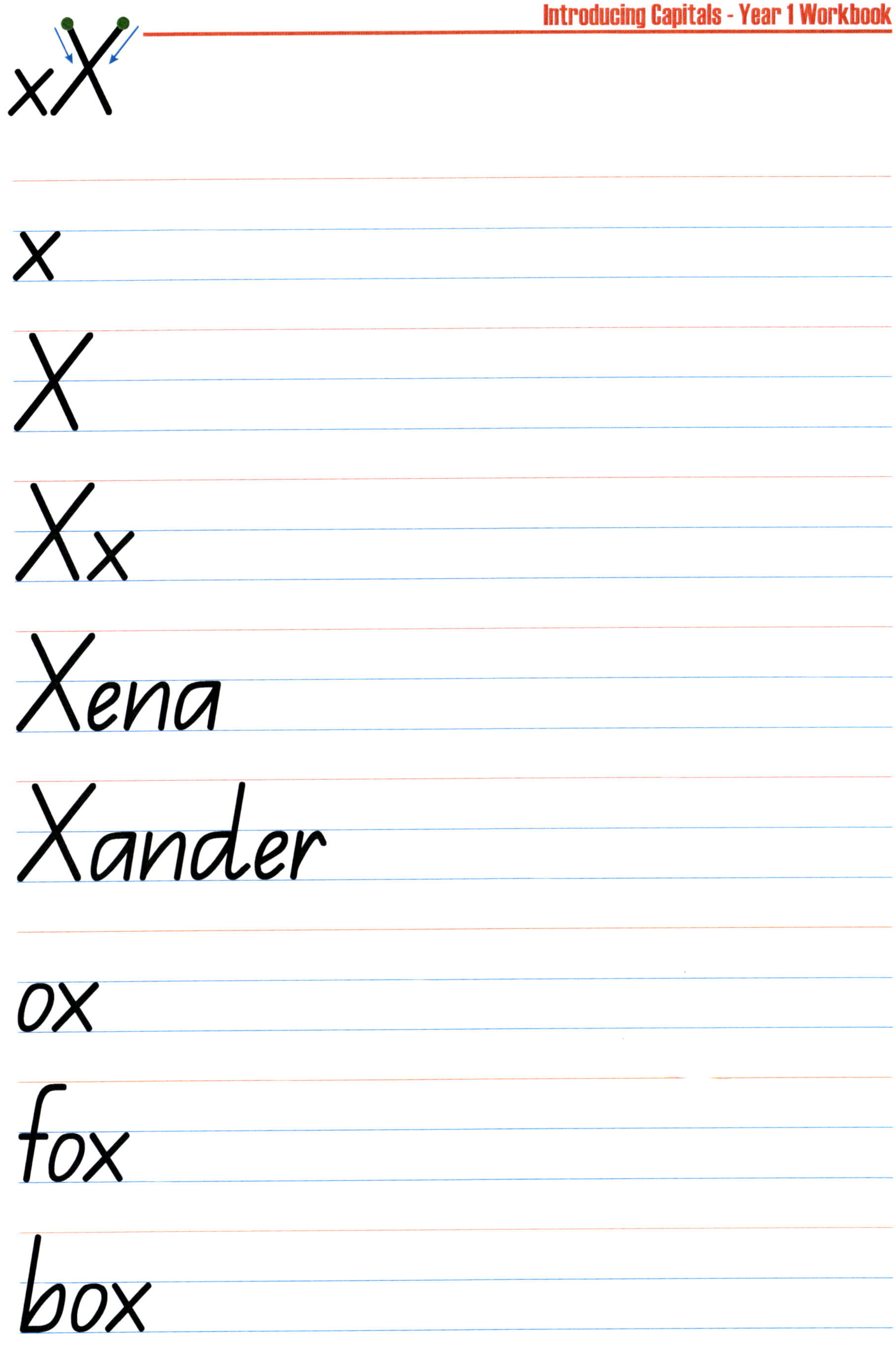
xX
x
X
Xx
Xena
Xander
ox
fox
box

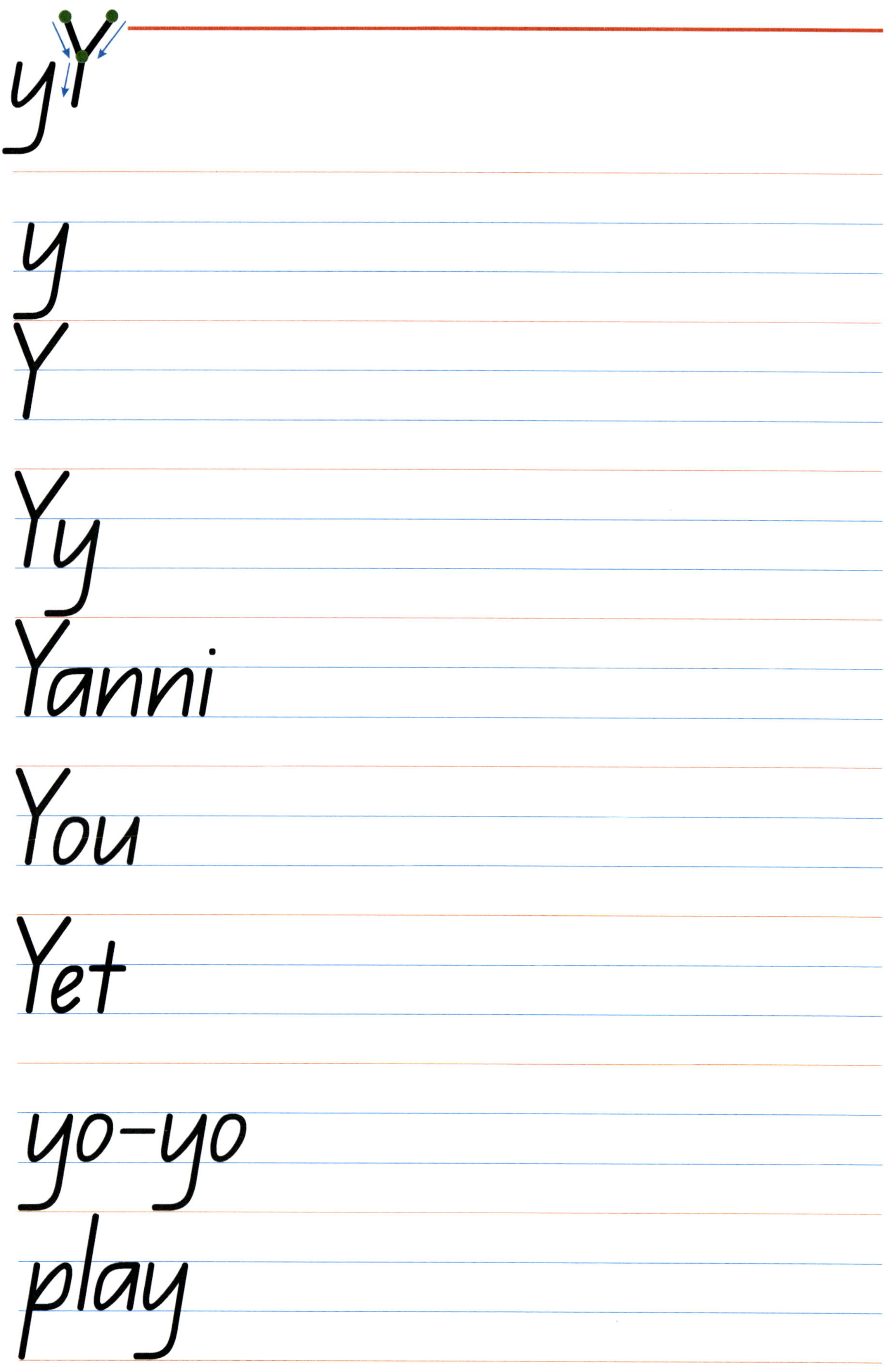
yY
y
Y
Yy
Yanni
You
Yet
yo-yo
play

s S

s

S

Ss

Susan

Sandi

bus

mess

Susan likes busses.

kK

k

K

Kk

Karen

Kay

Katrina

Black

Kevin is kind to Kate.

v V

v

V

Vv

Valerie

Verity

have

very

Valerie likes violets.

zZ

z

Z

Zz

Zac

Zara

zoo

zebra

Zac went to the zoo.